Teaching Online Without Losing Your Mind

Angela Velez-Solic, Ph.D.

To my husband, Brian,
for always being my biggest fan.

Table of Contents

Preface

What's inside?

1   Why am I doing this?   Page

- *How I got started*   2
- *Getting adequate preparation*   4
- *This isn't easy*   5
- *The transformational effect*   6

2   LMS, ELE, CMS? Oh my

- *Make your LMS your best friend*   8
- *Supplementing the LMS*   11
- *Your campus LMS person*   11
  should be a friend too
- *Chapter 2 checklist*   12

3   Time to be a student again

- *Training should be mandatory*   13
- *Experience and practice.*   14
  Repeat as necessary
- *Online is the only way*   15
- *Other effects of quality training*   16
- *Students are consumers & have choices*   17
- *If training isn't available in-house*   18
- *Training agenda items*   18
- *Chapter 3 checklist*   19

4   The drawing board

- *Start like this*   21
- *Instructional design suggestions*   22

- *You should create content too*   24
- *Weekly learning units*   25
- *Save directional content for last*   25
- *The personalization factor*   27
- *Chapter 4 checklist*   30

5   Make their time worth it

- *Project, problem, and case-based activities*   31
- *What about speeches, presentations, and language learners?*   37
- *Chapter 5 checklist*   39

6   Let's give 'em something to talk about

- *Interaction is vital*   40
- *Discussion question techniques*   41
- *One formula*   42
- *Discussion question examples*   43
- *Planning & managing discussions*   46
- *Grading discussions*   48
- *Being part of the interaction*   50
- *Chapter 6 checklist*   53

7   Assessment is a four-letter word

- *Start with objectives*   54
- *Traditional testing*   54
- *Testing integrity online*   56
- *Authentic assessment*   58
- *Chapter resources*   59
- *Chapter 7 checklist*   60

8   Give it some bling & make it sing

- *Pictures are worth 1000 words*   61
- *How to find tools & new things*   62
- *Inventory, then exploration*   63
- *Quantity & quality*   64

•	*ADA compliance*	*65*
•	*Browsers are wonky*	*66*
•	*Where do you get these?*	*66*
•	*Chapter 8 checklist*	*68*

9   It's SHOWTIME!

•	*Answering questions*	*70*
•	*Participating*	*71*
•	*Grading*	*72*
•	*Course maintenance*	*74*
•	*Low enrollment courses*	*75*
•	*Large enrollment courses*	*76*
•	*Chapter 9 checklist*	*78*

10   The dog ate my homework and I hate democrats

•	*Breaking the excuse machine*	*81*
•	*Other student issues*	*82*
	o *I'm stuck in my beliefs and everyone else is wrong*	*82*
	o *The overachiever*	*84*
	o *Habitual slacker*	*85*
	o *Hail the entitled one*	*87*
	o *Woefully underprepared*	*88*
	o *The plagiarizer*	*89*
•	*Chapter 10 checklist*	*91*

11   Ice cream sandwich anyone?

•	*The time factor*	*92*
•	*The sandwich method*	*93*
•	*Grading papers*	*94*
•	*Peer review helps*	*95*
•	*Chapter 11 checklist*	*98*

12   Growing pains

- *Potential course issues*   *100*
  and avoidance tactics
- *Chapter 12 checklist*   *103*

13   Just getting your feet wet

- *Getting started with blended learning*   *104*
- *How well do you like yours blended?*   *105*
- *Face to face time is crucial*   *106*
- *What you do online is important too*   *106*
- *It needs to be connected and make sense*   *107*
- *Using the "A" word again*   *108*
- *Chapter 13 checklist*   *110*

14   Ok, what now?

- *Hurray for online learning centers*   *111*
- *What about you, though?*   *113*
- *This can be an emotional experience*   *114*
- *Making changes*   *115*
- *What do the students think?*   *115*
- *Keep learning, experimenting, and sharing*   *116*
- *Concluding thoughts*   *117*
- *Chapter 14 checklist*   *118*

Acknowledgements   **118**

About the Author   **120**

References   **121**

Image credits   **122**

Preface

I've always wanted to write a book and publish it. This is not my first book, mind you. I've written a novel, three children's books, and a book-length poetry manuscript. I never tried to publish any of them, at least not yet. This book is different, though. I came up with this idea after I spent some time on Amazon searching for books about online teaching and course design. I love some of the books already out there and greatly respect the authors who published them, yet I found the resources lacking in a few areas. I was looking for a book that was more of a step-by-step guide, a book that is realistic and raw, funny but very serious, a book that told the whole truth about the reality of designing your own online course and then teaching it for the first time. I couldn't find it.

So, I had an epiphany that moment! I remember it very clearly- the summer of 2013 (one year ago as a matter of fact, to the very moment that I am writing this preface). I felt a surge of excitement, the shake of adrenaline in my fingers at the realization that I knew enough to write that very book and knew that people would want it, would need it, and I could fulfill my dream of publishing a book while also helping to make the world a better place (at least for faculty members who teach online and the online students who take their awesome courses). I also remember at that very moment opening a Word document and starting the first chapter. I couldn't stop. When I was done I smiled and my heart beat crazy in my chest. I felt like I was doing something important and life altering.

Throughout this past year I have done a lot of work in my field, spent many hours at conferences, networked with people from around the world, sought the advice of my good friends from IELOL (the Institute for Engaged Leadership in Online Learning, which is a joint effort between Penn State and the Online Learning Consortium, formerly known as Sloan-C), my friends and colleagues from the OLC mentioned previously, coworkers at

Indiana University, and other colleagues from other institutions. I talked to as many people as I could, continued to grow and nurture my professional network, and tirelessly swam with the fast-flowing current of online teaching, learning, and technological innovation. I have to, or I will no longer be relevant and useful in my field.

I wrote this book whenever I could. I am a natural writer (I've taught English for a long time and started writing when I was a little kid and stapled loose leaf pieces of lined paper together to make my own books), so I wrote quickly. The words just flowed from my mind to my fingers like warm maple syrup over hot pancakes. I read a few chapters to my husband who listened intently but whom I knew really didn't 'get it'. That's ok, though, he always gave me pats on the back anyway. I can't describe to you what it feels like to have an idea, start making it happen, and finally see a finished product. It's euphoric; I'm happy that you're part of my joy!

What's inside?

I will tell you right now that if you're looking for a book filled with endless, properly formatted APA citations of people who support what it is I am telling you, this is not **that** book. I have very few citations in here because they don't matter. Well, they **do** matter because research in this field is in its infancy and those who do publish quality writing should be respected and their books, articles, blogs, and other materials are important contributions to our fundamental and academic understanding of what is happening in higher education, but you need to trust that I know this stuff enough to teach you without them.

I have strong opinions and you will read a lot of them: about faculty training, about what 'quality' is, about active and engaging online learning, about practical application being the pinnacle of a good learning experience, and a few other things. I feel qualified to judge these areas of online learning and can support my assertions. I am not a traditionalist when it comes to education and I never will be. I don't think kids should sit in desks all day and learn, and don't agree with standardized tests and measurements of intelligence. I don't say those things in this book because they're irrelevant, but I have been an educator for a long enough time to know in which philosophies I am grounded and which I will continue to preach. While I say I'm not a traditionalist, there are still parts of me that refuse to acquiesce to the trends. I prefer to read a book rather than a screen, for example. So, while I work with technology and significantly depend on it, I still hold on to some 'old ways' of doing things.

My approach is informal. I will tell you like it is, how it is, and what to expect. This is who I am as a person; I'm very much unrestrained and uninterested in being the most politically correct person in the room. I am, however, interested in honesty and forthrightness, which is painfully missing in the academy, I might add. Anyway, I give you personal stories and experiences as well as examples from my own courses. I tell you to contact me, and I sincerely mean it.

The book begins with how I personally got involved with online learning and then moves into the process of planning the online course on paper (like a blue print), deciding on activities, discussion and interaction, how you're going to assess their learning, adding some bells and whistles, and then moves into what happens when it's time to go live and teach it for the first time. After that I cover some student issues, feedback strategies, and what to do when things don't go well. Towards the end I have a chapter that covers hybrid or blended approaches, which is its own animal all together. One of my peer reviewers felt like that chapter didn't fit with the rest of the book, but it's important enough to me to keep it despite the fact that it might seem oddly 'thrown in'. Finally, I wrap it up with some ideas moving forward.

Within the chapters I do have some links and if you have the print version I do apologize for you not having the ability to touch your finger on the word or words to magically see that link. However, I'd bet my bottom dollar that we will have that capability at some point, when anything and everything we see could be hyperlinked. For now, what you will need to do in those situations is simply use Google, or your search engine of choice, to look it up online until that technology is invented. What you will see, though, is this symbol:★ and when you do, know that it's a helpful tip for you to remember or take note of. Hint, highlight it! I've also included end-of-chapter checklists for you in most of the chapters, just to remind you of some important tidbits from that chapter.

In this book I hope you find some help, epiphanies, comic relief, and recognition that you're not alone in this adventure that is online teaching. I look forward to hearing from my readers about what worked, what didn't, and perhaps new ideas I can include in future iterations. Thanks for taking the time to read this and, if you like what you see, please pass it on to others.

Respectfully yours,

Angela

1

Why am I doing this?

Some people embraced online education back in the day when it was quite taboo. If people heard you earned a degree online they were very likely to laugh at you and consider you a slacker, someone unable to handle 'real' learning at a 'real' university. Times have changed and while that attitude can still be heard through some ivory halls and posted throughout the Internet here and there, generally speaking online courses and degrees are getting a lot less negative attention. This is likely due to the fact that research has been widely published in the last five years or so that shows that academic rigor can be part of the

I. Kobylanski / Flickr

online learning experience; in fact, some studies have even shown online learning as better than traditional learning in some circumstances.

Perhaps you were an early adopter of this new type of educating. Perhaps you scoffed at it early on, and are just starting to consider its viability. Maybe you're still a naysayer and someone has encouraged you to learn more about it because you are an expert at what you know and they want you to offer an online class (much to your chagrin and you're kicking and screaming at the very idea of it all).

It doesn't matter where you fit on that pendulum. I hope that this book offers you some practical advice from start to finish so that regardless of your personal beliefs about online learning, after you read this book you will be able to create a spectacular online course worthy of awards and accolades (you can feel free to write to me if this, in fact, does happen-- I will be proud of you).

How I got started:

It might surprise you, but I was also one of those people who turned my nose up at online degrees. I remember one example in particular (and in retrospect I am very ashamed of this). It was 1995 and I was in my junior year at Grand Valley State University in Michigan. My boyfriend's roommate was earning his MBA online from a popular for-profit university and when I was asked about it (since I was studying to be a teacher at the time), I said judgmental things like "I guess he just can't get in anywhere else", and "It must be so hard (sarcasm) to go to college online (more sarcasm)." I earned my teaching degree and 6 months later started graduate school. In 1998 I began my own teaching career in the dark halls of basement classrooms at Purdue Calumet in Hammond, Indiana.

A few years later I started teaching at an urban school called Westwood College of Technology and, again, found myself in basement classrooms (strange irony there). In 2005 I moved a bit far from the college and instead of quitting they asked if I was interested in teaching online for Westwood College Online. I'm sure my face scrunched up in a "You can't be serious" expression. After all, I was such an involved, animated, participatory instructor who enjoyed the one on one time, face-to-face time, and valuable verbal and non-verbal communication, not to mention the relationships I developed with my students. How on earth could I be the teacher I knew I was without being IN a classroom in front of an audience of (mostly) transfixed faces?

Because of life circumstances at that time, I decided to give it a try. I'm generally a risk taker as it is, and other than weird foods, deep water, or activities involving high altitudes (like above 12 feet), I'll probably try anything once. One of my many convictions is that people should avoid judging anything without experiencing it for themselves. I went through a mandatory training and was given an English course that was already pre-designed for me. All I had to do was participate in the course and assess my students. How hard could that be, right? Overall I had a very positive experience, both learning as an online student (while training), and being an online instructor. I was so surprised that the words I used with my students conveyed my personality probably just as effectively as I did when I was standing in front of the class flailing my arms as I spoke. It only took a few semesters before I realized that I was very, very wrong about my inexperienced judgments about online learning.

I will admit something more to you-- in 2005 I was supporting myself and 4 very young children on a meager, I-don't-know-if-I-can-feed-my-kids adjunct teaching salary ($16,500.00 that year, I looked it up), and a close friend and confidant warned me that I would not find a full time teaching job at a university without having a terminal degree. However, I had to be realistic and accept the fact that my youngest child was still in diapers, I didn't have any money for child care, was in the throes of a very ugly divorce without a child support order, and needed to teach as many courses as I could in order to survive. How would I fit doctoral studies in considering everything else on my plate? Even though I knew online learning could be high quality, and knew that diploma mills weren't the only institutions offering online degrees, I was still afraid to earn my own degree that way, especially since I had earned two degrees very traditionally.

As much as I was worried about how it would be viewed later, I enrolled in an online Ph.D. program in early 2006. I am a very honest person, and I will tell you that undoubtedly I learned more during those 4 ½ years than I did during my traditional master's degree program. Online learning for me, as a very self-motivated learner, worked and worked well. I knew I would have to prove myself once I finished, but I've been able to do that just fine and, as far as I know, my online Ph.D. has not affected my ability to land a really great job nor has it affected the respect I've earned in the field.

The point of that personal story is that online learning provides access to students who are not able to attend a traditional campus due to life circumstances. Of course, some students choose to take online courses even if they are more than capable of sitting in a traditional classroom, some because they think it's easier, some because they prefer to learn 'alone', some because they'd like to save gas and time, and some because they learn better that way. The access part is key; I know if it weren't for online learning and the quality education I received I certainly wouldn't be writing this book nor would I have had the opportunities for leadership and teaching that I have had in my career. Can you imagine what earning a college degree would be like for someone who has dreamed of it, but didn't have access? This is one really good reason to invest your time and academic talents to develop excellent online courses.

You're not reading this to get my personal stories, but I can't help myself and because I see so much educational value in stories, you will hear more as you read on. You're reading this because you want to learn how to design an online class and do it the best way you can, right? I hope this is the case because online learning can vary in quality from absolute crap (such as courses that are nothing more than glorified correspondence courses) to spectacular works of instructional design genius and everywhere in between. Aim your sights at somewhere in between, but if you do become a course design genius, come back and teach me a thing or two, will you?

What seems to set quality courses apart from the I-can't-believe-students-paid-for-that type of online courses is the type of preparation the instructor had before he or she designed and taught the course. Again, I speak from experience here. Many universities still do not require any sort of pre-requisite training of their faculty members before telling them, "Hey, by the way, you're going to teach this English 101 course online next semester" and expecting them to create a quality course and know how to navigate an online teaching environment as if it's natural.

Getting adequate preparation:

If you ask me my opinion (who am I kidding, even if you don't ask me my opinion) I will tell you that it's not acceptable to offer online courses without requiring proper training. To me, it's like allowing a mechanic who has only worked on cars to work on my motorcycle. Will he do it right? Maybe. After all, the person is a mechanic, right? Would I feel better riding down the highway knowing an actual trained motorcycle mechanic fixed the leak in my primary? Probably. The same metaphor can be used here. While educators know their subject, knowing how to teach in a new environment requires training and experience.

I know it's hard to convince you (if you're a faculty member) to do anything sometimes, but teaching you HOW to do this online teaching stuff is imperative to quality online teaching. I will explain more about training in Chapter 3. Universities that are for-profit almost always require training (unpaid), but also do not require instructors to design their own courses. They have teams of people to do that- usually at least one subject matter expert (also referred to as SME), at least one instructional designer, and possibly a technology person or administrator. The idea of pre-designed courses is a subject I will not debate in this book, but the value of pre-designed courses is that instructors can spend their time interacting, teaching, assessing, and providing feedback without worrying about content issues. The negative, of course, is lack of academic freedom and ability to modify content.

This isn't easy:

Since you're in this to design your own course, the above situation probably doesn't apply, at least not unless you will be moonlighting as an adjunct somewhere else later on. What's important to keep in mind is that this will take some time, and it should. While it's lovely to teach in your jammies, or from the beach in Aruba, or even on an airplane over the Alps, you have to get the course designed first. It's a very popular myth to the people who have not yet experienced online teaching first hand that it doesn't take time and those who do it are taking the 'easy' way out of their teaching responsibilities. Anyone who has done this will emphatically deny the fact that it's any less work. As a matter of fact, you're pretty much teaching 24/7. Even if you're not 'IN' your online course, your essence is there, your students are there, and learning is going on. Online faculty members have to spend a lot of time balancing the urge to be there while the learning is going on with other life, teaching, and departmental responsibilities.

I will be honest and tell you that once you've designed a course, taught it, and made the revisions you needed to it's easier the second and subsequent times because you don't need to invest that upfront time. However, the courses do not teach themselves, and if they do, then it's not being done correctly. That's actually a myth-- that once a faculty member designs the course, all they have to do is grade and the students go about the business of learning the content without faculty participation in that learning experience. Again, it does happen that way in bad cases, but that is not what quality instructors do. We will talk about that more in Chapter 9 (feel free to skip ahead if you so choose).

Another reality is that you're still going to need to deal with student issues. You're still going to have excuses (probably more because of the distance between you and them provides that buffer), and students are going to try your patience. You will still have students who are M.I.A, and those who plagiarize, and those who try to do the bare minimum just to get by. However, because everything is in writing, and because you will have a loop-hole-free syllabus (thanks to learning how to do that through this book), you can always just defer to it and the contract they signed (you'll learn about that too). It's wonderful that everything is there at all times, so you don't have to deal with landmines of student issues as long as you do the prep work in advance. In any case, I will delve into the student "issues" subject in chapter 11.

A really wonderful reality that you will find exciting is that your course will have a very awesome dynamic as long as you follow these suggestions. You will find that your students will dig deeper into the content, they will talk more (because they'll be forced to, really, but also because you'll give them things to talk about that they will WANT to discuss), and engage in learning much more often than 90 minutes on Tuesdays and Thursdays or whatever class time you might have if you've been teaching it face-to-face.

The transformational effect:

Amy / Flickr

It's time for another story. At one university where I worked I made a presentation at a departmental meeting. I hadn't been there very long and, after the presentation, a "very experienced" faculty member sat in a chair, leaned back with his thick arms tightly bound across his chest and asked me this, "How do you feel about your role in dehumanizing the educational experience for students?" I'm very serious. This really happened. Fortunately I came up with some witty, yet polite answer because a week after that this award-winning professor who had taught for longer than I was alive contacted me. He said he gave it some thought and he wanted to take my online teaching course. I told my boss and he wondered if it was some kind of joke. I couldn't help but wonder if I was going to be part of some experiment. However, I took him at face value and enrolled him, and had to spend an hour in his office showing him how to log in to Blackboard since he hadn't ever logged into the learning management system.
Did you read that clearly?
Not ever.

He struggled the first week, but after that he got the hang of it and participated fully, completed all of the assignments, and graduated as one of my special students! The next semester I was surprised when he busted into my office, his cheeks pink with enthusiasm, and exclaimed for the whole center to hear that he used discussion boards for the first time with his face-to-face class and he couldn't believe what his students were doing. He said, "Why haven't I done this before? I can't believe I haven't done this in all my years of teaching!" I was beaming with pride like a mother when her child takes his or her first steps. He was so excited that the next semester he used discussions in all of his courses and the third semester after he completed my online teaching course he started designing his own online course. I consulted with him periodically and it shocked so many people that this man who thought online learning was "the devil of academe" taught his very own online course in the Fall of 2012 (and did a mighty fine job of it too).

That long diatribe was written to exemplify that while online learning, MOOCs, and all things virtual are threats, in some respects, to the traditions of teaching and learning, they have a place in the world. Online learning can be so reflective and transformational that you too will wonder why you haven't embraced this sooner. When done well, students can, and do, learn more online than they do sitting in the desks of a lecture hall-- for a lot of reasons. I am here to help you learn how to create the highest quality learning environments for your students without delving into theory and research findings because I've spent many years doing that. I know this stuff and I know why it works. I've read the research and everything I am telling you in this book can be validated by the research. I promise I will not lead you astray. Now let's get started.

2

LMS, ELE, CMS? Oh my

Your institution likely purchased a license to a LMS, which stands for Learning Management System. Sometimes people refer to this as a CMS, or Course Management System. One faculty member who I used to work with liked to use the word ELE or Enhanced Learning Environment. I really like that idea and perhaps it will take off if enough people read this book. If so, cite Jane Peller from Northeastern Illinois University, a retired Social Work Professor extraordinaire! At any rate, these acronyms refer to the virtual environment in which students and educators find themselves when learning takes place outside a brick and mortar classroom. Some of these systems are Desire to Learn (D2L), Blackboard, Canvas, Moodle, Sakai, and many others. It is likely your institution has one of them.

Make your LMS your best friend:

It's very important for you to become intimately familiar with your own LMS. It's best to start using it slowly versus jumping feet first and trying to use every tool available to you. Doing it that way could become overwhelming really fast. Each institution has its own LMS administrator or administrators who decide what is on the navigation bar when you or the students log in.

D. Medina / Morguefile

Sometimes that navigation bar cannot be modified (mostly true for for-profit institutions that provide courses that are already designed) or other institutions that provide you with a course that someone else designed. For many institutions, though, that navigation bar comes pre-designed, but you can modify the order of the tools, remove the ones you don't use, or add what you need to add.

Make sure you know what's available to you in the LMS so you know how to plan your online course. For example, some LMSs like

Canvas and later forms of Blackboard provide modularized content. That is, all of your content for a week, unit, or chapter is on one page. Make sure you know how content is organized because that will affect your planning. In addition to presenting content like lectures, videos, presentations, notes, directions, etc., there are also built in collaboration tools.

All systems have built in discussion tools. Most of them are called 'discussion boards', while occasionally they're called 'forums'. It's necessary to learn how to create forums, discussion threads, how to read, respond, and grade discussions. Think of a forum like a room where you're having a dinner party. You speak to the whole room and give them something to talk about. Then, the discussion threads are like the responses that each person gives to that topic or question you posed—like how people at a dinner party tend to talk in small groups in various areas of the home. Typically online courses will have a discussion forum for each week or unit. Courses that are strongly quantitative might have a little bit less discussion than one forum for each unit. Speaking of quantitative courses, even when the subject of a course is math or statistics, discussions can be utilized. It just takes some creativity to come up with questions that can get students 'talking'.

Besides discussion tools, other interactive tools that systems have are wikis, blogs, and possibly some synchronous tools. Wikis are great if you want your students to work together to create something, perhaps a book chapter, an informational document, or 'pretend' website. If you've seen Wikipedia, that's what a wiki is, a place for people to create a site full of information about a subject that users can edit at any given time. When Wikis are part of the LMS, the instructor has access to who added what and when so that it's easy to grade participation.

Blogs are slightly different and offer students a chance to post something that's important to them, and other students can comment. It's wonderful for lessons on argument and persuasion. The students can include images, links, and text. Even if the LMS does not have a built-in Wiki or Blog tool, there are free versions of these out on the web that can be used and added to your course with ease. Seek out your IT professional or instructional design person to help you with this.

Synchronous tools are typically not included in an LMS. There are tools, however, that institutions can purchase such as Blackboard

Collaborate, Adobe Connect, and others. These tools are easily embedded in your online course and offer you an opportunity to meet with your students live (or synchronously, meaning at the same time). The tools allow you to have a white board (you can write on it and so can students), a web-browsing tool, a presentation tool (to upload Power Points or other presentations), and some even have video. Students can chat with each other while you're talking to them, you can give them real-time surveys, and have them collaborate in break out groups too. These tools can be expensive, but there are free tools out there as long as your class isn't too large. Please be careful using synchronous activities. Students take online classes for various reasons, one of which is flexibility. Requiring students to be online at a specific time on a specific day defeats the purpose and it is nearly impossible to choose a day/time that works for everyone. It can be useful for optional activities.

Aesthetically, LMSs can be fairly dull. Thankfully some of them allow customization with color and even course banners. If you are a Blackboard institution, you can create a simple course banner using Power Point! ★ Seriously-- all you do is open a PPT, choose a theme you want, then go to File>Page Setup and change the size to approximately 5" wide by 3" tall (you can play with these sizes if you want). Then, put your course name in the slide and save it first as a PPT (so you can change it later for a different semester) and then save it again as a .jpg file (File>Save As>jpg).

Then, go into the course customization link on the lower left side in a course and select 'style' then upload the .jpg banner. Voila, instant 'wow' when the students log in! What I do is change the color of my navigation background to match my banner colors so it all looks like it goes together. One word of wisdom that I learned the hard way- don't include the semester or any dates in your banner image. Just put the course name/number and title. This way you can re-use it. A word of caution, though, your LMS might be locked down for branding purposes, so you may not be able to customize your course look and feel.

In addition to making a banner, you can add images throughout the course too. Most of the systems have the ability to do that. I like to find copyright free, creative commons images so I don't get sued or don't make the IT department worry. I also use a site called Morgue File. Just use a search engine to find it. Those images at Morgue File are really large, so when you save them I would advise you to resize them to make adding them to your content areas and even announcements a lot easier.

Supplementing the LMS:

You don't have to use JUST the tools that your LMS provides for you unless your institution has a policy against using third party tools, which are basically things your institution hasn't purchased or doesn't support. Before you get too excited about the tools I tell you about, please go ask someone who would know whether or not it's ok. Generally it probably is, but the IT support folks may tell you that you're on your own in terms of support and problem solving.

There are so many free tools out on the web that you can use alongside your LMS to make the learning experience so much richer for your students. I have a list of many of these tools that I try to update on a regular basis. I won't list them here because they change so quickly that I don't want an outdated document associated with this book. Instead, I invite you to send me an email (justcallmeang@hotmail.com) to ask me for the "bells and whistles" document and I will send it to you★. I will include some of them later (Chapter 9, Give it some Bling!), but I will make the disclaimer that I cannot promise that a tool won't be dead, not free any more, or changed in any way since this book was published.

Sebastiano / Morguefile

What's nice about these tools is that so many of them can just embed right in the LMS, so your students can play learning games right within your content without leaving the course, they can watch videos, take anonymous, real-time surveys, and much more! Learn how to 'embed' something with html coding. Don't be scared, it's not difficult to do. Your university's instructional technologist or IT person can help.

Your campus LMS person should be a friend too:

There's a lot to learn about your LMS and how to make it work best for you and your courses. It's a great idea to become good friends with the LMS administrators on your campus, even if it's just one person, make friends with him or her. Bring cupcakes. You don't need to suffer through not understanding how to work your LMS because there's a person who can help you. Find out who that is and introduce yourself. That person is probably very busy and overwhelmed at times (trust me, I've been that person) so your kindness and appreciation will go a long way.

Chapter 2 Checklist: The LMS

- o   Can the navigation bar be changed?
- o   What tools are available in your LMS?
- o   What can you use to modularize content?
- o   Are any synchronous communication tools available?
- o   Can you customize your LMS look?
- o   Are third party tools allowed (like using web tools to enhance my course)?
- o   Who is the campus LMS person or people?
- o   Get to know the people just mentioned (really well)

3

Time to be a student again

I cannot stress it enough that if you are asked to teach online, or just want to, you need to be properly prepared to do so. I know that it might feel demeaning to consider 'training' for something, especially if you're a well-educated professor who's been teaching for 20 years and have dozens of publications and other trophies of academic success. Most professors have never been taught HOW to teach, have they? They learn their subject, they master it, study it, write about it, publish it, lecture about it, and teach others what they know through telling and *sometimes* showing and doing. However, unless you're in the field of education, you probably haven't taken courses on *how* to teach students effectively. I find this very problematic because I've experienced poor teaching in my own learning, and I see poor teaching in the halls of my university, as well as in the virtual classrooms of underprepared instructors.

Training should be mandatory:

Yes, I used the "M" word. In an ideal world any person who wishes to teach at a university should take a course or two in andragogy, feedback, and assessment. However, I know that this probably won't happen in my lifetime. Instructors who want to teach online, though, should be required to take mandatory training to learn how to adjust to a virtual learning environment that is available 24/7 to the students.

kconnors / Morguefile

What I've seen happen is traditional institutions that have been behind the curveball and that entered online learning later in the game did so without a great deal of thought as to how it would happen. They assigned online courses to faculty members with the hope that as long as they're technologically savvy that they will know how to design, teach, and manage a course, not to mention fit a constantly changing learning environment into their teaching, research and service load as well as their personal life. How did that work for them, you think? Were the courses excellent? Did students praise these instructors? Did the faculty members feel like they knew what they were doing? Did they want to do it again?

I want to take a moment and give you some props, though, for getting this book. I don't know your personal situation, but if you happen to be someone who doesn't have a solid training program at your institution, reading this book says a lot about your personal dedication to learning how to navigate, create, and teach in this new environment. Maybe you've been told to get this book by a trainer or instructional design group at your institution and, if so, please tell them thank you and how awesome they are for choosing my book to supplement what they're doing.

Experience and practice. Repeat as necessary:

Ginucplathottam / Morguefile

I'm going to use the metaphor of the motorcycle again-- probably because spring is around the corner and that means riding season is too. Let's imagine that you decide that you're feeling uncool. You're feeling like you don't take enough risks and you want to change that, so you decide to buy your own motorcycle. Then you're offered two ways to learn how to ride. Out of those two ways, you pick the cautious approach and someone takes you to a classroom, plays videos about how to work the motorcycle, how to shift, how to avoid collisions, and what to do when something goes wrong. Then, you go outside and your instructor says, "Now, go ride it."

What do you think you would do? Would you be confident? That's doubtful. Why? I will answer for you since I can't hear what you're saying. It's because you did not get any real practice DOING or

EXPERIENCING it. What will you need to do to be able to ride it without landing in an emergency room? You will need someone to **show** you. You will need **experience** and **practice**. I understand that you may not have control over this whatsoever and decisions about how and to what extent the faculty is trained tend to be made from the top down. Perhaps you can share this part of the book with a person who has influence over these policies to encourage them down a specific path towards faculty training in an online environment.

I strongly discourage any training for online teaching that does not take place online, the environment in which you will be teaching. While face-to-face training is better than no training at all, it's not even close to the same thing as experiencing it as a student. It forces you to get a little uncomfortable, feel a change of role that you likely haven't experienced in a long time; it puts you on a level playing field with others who might be adjuncts or lecturers who are learning with you online. That is ok because it is within that discomfort and disorientation that you will learn the most and it will make you a better designer and teacher.

Online is the only way:

I really want to drive this home- especially if you are the person in charge or the person who can influence the person in charge of designing faculty training. It should be online because the experience of being an online student is priceless for instructors. As an online student, you get a perspective that will inevitably stick in the back of your mind when you're teaching your own class. I've experienced many different online training programs-- many were at for-profit institutions and others at community colleges and private universities. I've also designed three of them, and taught so many I can't even count right now, so I consider myself an expert in this area. Part of my dissertation covered online faculty training as well. All of these training courses served the same purpose, but some achieved the objectives better than others.

Training has other benefits too. You will find that if you are an experienced online instructor with training you can show evidence of, there's money to be made teaching online outside of your institution (and there *is* money to be made, just so you know), you will find that most institutions, and **all** for-profits require unpaid training. They last from 4 to 6 weeks typically and can be very time consuming. The training generally deals with their LMS, how to use the functions of it, their requirements of online instructors, and how to deal with the various issues faced in virtual classrooms like grading, feedback, problematic students, etc. Unfortunately, a lot of it is unnecessary busy work to weed out the 'weak' and undedicated.

If your institution does not provide training for its instructors, suggest it to someone. Most Centers for Teaching & Learning provide this service as long as they have someone on staff that is experienced and able to design and teach a course of this nature. This person should be experienced in instructional design, should have experience as an instructor in online environments, and should be able to model excellence in online teaching. It is even better to have someone in this position who has also been a traditional faculty member who can speak to that shift that happens when one goes from face to face to online teaching. Call it having street 'cred' if you want, but it is helpful in influencing faculty and having them feel comfortable with that person 'teaching' them.

Other effects of quality online training:

What ends up happening is this type of course brings professors together from various disciplines and unites them with a common mission, which is to learn how to design stellar online courses and become acceptable, if not excellent online teachers. They will discuss with each other, problem solve, share experiences, and become their own learning community.

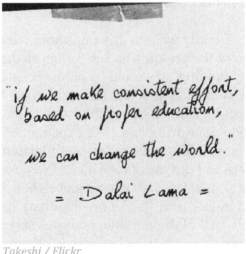

"if we make consistent effort, based on proper education, we can change the world."

= Dalai Lama =

Takeshi / Flickr

What also happens is that they become better educators in their face-to-face courses. I have seen this happen hundreds of times. It's an unexpected consequence of online faculty training. Julia Parra (2010) studied this phenomenon and wrote a dissertation about it and I, along with a fellow IU Northwest faculty member, studied it as well (Velez-Solic & Kilibarda, 2015). It's amazing what training can do as long as it's designed properly and taught by qualified, experienced, excellent faculty.

Another result is that your university can create this cadre of faculty members with the SAME experience in faculty training, who are taught the SAME things about quality design, student engagement, assessment, feedback, and instructor presence and then, after some time, you have a bunch of interest in online teaching and those courses will have a similar flavor. I don't mean the courses will be the same; that won't happen unless the institution subscribes to a pre-designed course model (all for-profits do this and some private institutions). What it means is at least all of the faculty members who went through training with the same instructor have been given a consistent message.

Students are consumers and have choices:

There's an inherent problem for 'late to the game' institutions when students can pick and choose where to learn. After all, they have so many choices now in higher education- online learning has earned a decent reputation and even some for-profits have quality online programs. If they find themselves at a university that's local with a good reputation, but with online courses that range from boring content with missing-without-action faculty members to really intense, really work-laden courses, that lack of knowing what to expect would be scary. So, if faculty members get a consistent message about how to design and teach online, the students will be much better off and more likely to stick with their programs instead of jumping ship to an online school that will offer them a better experience, even if it means a much higher cost.

When it comes to this training stuff, you're bound to find faculty members who think much too highly of themselves and who will shake their incredibly intelligent heads at the very thought of it. That's ok, to each his own. I would caution department chairs and Deans from choosing these faculty members to teach online courses. It's not because they don't know their subjects, because I am certain they do, but those who are not willing to participate in a training program because they feel like they already know what to do probably won't do a very good job at it. Those are fightin' words, I know, but experience has taught me a thing or two about the best people to sit behind the screen with online students and it's not the ones who are arrogant and unwilling to be learners themselves.

If training isn't available in-house:

If you do not have training available at your institution, consider taking training elsewhere. The two organizations that offer online teaching training with which I am familiar are the Online Learning Consortium (formerly Sloan-C) and The Illinois Online Network (ION). I have taught the OLC Certificate program for online teaching (which is a 9 week course plus electives) and know the man behind ION (as of the time of this writing it is Scott Johnson). You can look these up and see if either will work for you. I would bring this to the attention of the person with the proverbial checkbook to see if the institution would be willing to put you through a training or certificate program. A great benefit to an outside program is that you get to mingle with people from all over the world and share experiences; a caveat is that you are probably going to be learning on an LMS (remember what that stands for?) that is not familiar and you won't learn how to use your own to its best potential.

Training agenda items:

In my opinion, the best type of training will provide you with a checklist to complete a design of your own course. Your institution might subscribe to Quality Matters, the Blackboard Exemplary course rubric, The OLC Pillars of Quality, the Chico rubric, or something else built internally. I will cover these in a later chapter, by the way. I like to provide assignments that are actual activities you do in your own course (or a possible future online course) that gets you on your way. So, when the 4 weeks is over, you might have little bits and pieces of an online course already created!

The training should also help prepare you for situations you might (ok, let's be real, you WILL) encounter in an online class. I like to do this through class discussions. For example, how will you discourage cheating (especially if your class is quantitative in nature and does not lend itself well to written assignments or authentic projects)? How will you deal with student excuses (because lots of people can die in a family, especially if that student is not in your local area and is never on campus)? What about issues of diversity and ESL? What can you do to help create an immediate feeling of community and connection? When you're in a course with other faculty members, you will learn from them and get ideas that you haven't considered before. Even after these many years of faculty training, and hundreds upon hundreds of faculty members trained, I still learn something new each time I teach a training course. I think it's amazing.

Chapter 3 Checklist: Training

- o   Does your institution offer training to teach online?
- o   Look for the person or people who are responsible for online 'stuff'
- o   Do you have any instructional designers?
- o   Find out how to get help from these people (if they're available)
- o   Needing training is not a bad thing
- o   Learning online is the best way to learn how to be an online teacher
- o   People who learn how to teach online become better face-to-face teachers
- o   Online is not the enemy, but it is what students want
- o   Online teaching is not for everyone and should not be forced on anyone
- o   Other professional development is offered through the Online Learning Consortium and the Illinois Online Network

4

The drawing board

UNDER
CONSTRUCTION

OPENING
AUGUST

I. Richter / Flickr

So, you've been given an online class to design and teach in a future semester. You know the title, the section number, and the learning objectives. You have a LMS and a general course navigation set up that comes with every shell created by the IT team. I will not assume here that you've taken a training course. So if this information is too basic for you, move on, Smarty-Pants, until you find something that helps you.

I will admit to you that even after designing dozens (I should probably count them one of these days so I can quit playing it safe and using generalities) of courses, I still get a little overwhelmed when I see a new course that needs designing. Want to know something? I was once asked to assist a faculty member (who I did not know) at a university (where I did not work) to design an online class (in something with which I was unfamiliar). At first I felt nervous and apprehensive. I know what it feels like to be a little uneasy, and even uncertain despite knowing full well I am capable of doing this. So, don't feel bad if you do feel a little bit freaked out.

Before I get into the specific instructions, please understand that these basic design suggestions can be applied to any level of any kind of course. They can be used in K-12 all the way through graduate courses. If you want to make the words or categories more sophisticated, that's fine. Also, for skill-based courses such as math, finance, accounting and the like, discussions and interactivity can be difficult to think about, but not impossible. The interaction might play a lesser role than in other disciplines, but it should have some part in the course. So, please do not automatically remove it from your planning sheet if you teach a course like that.

20

Start like this:

I like to start off low tech in the very beginning. In order to make this easier for you to follow, I will put this in bullet points.

- Get a piece of paper or a few sheets of paper. At the top of one of them write the objectives of that course, specifically the course-level objectives.

- Then, write Week 1, Week 2, etc. until you've covered all of the weeks available (6, 8, 10, 12, 16, etc.). Make sure that under each week you leave ample space to write some notes.

- If you will be having a midterm project, exam, or paper, indicate within which week you will have that.

- Look at your school's calendar. Note the dates of the weeks on your papers and indicate any holidays off. Just because students learn online doesn't mean they have to work over holidays ☺

- Note any final exam/final project week

- Now it's time to figure out weekly objectives. These could be taken from the textbook you use (steal the objectives from the chapters, but make sure they align with the course objectives). Each week, write down what they should know by the end of that week. If you want to break your course into units or chapters, that's fine too. Weeks seem to be easier to manage.

- Once you have your objectives, think about how you will measure them. I do not encourage you to have more than 2 items each week that you have to manually grade. If you have 2 manually graded items and one LMS graded item (like a multiple choice/true false quiz), it's fine, but do not overload the students or yourself.

- Then consider what the students will do to reach those objectives. What will they read? What will they do? Write down some ideas.

- You should include weekly interaction with your students. This is typically done on the discussion boards or forums. This is not something you should take lightly nor something you do without careful design. I will teach you more about this in Chapter 6. For some courses that allow for it (like writing/literature/English), I have peer review weeks instead of discussion.

- Fill out as much as you can for each week of the course. If you don't use a textbook you might have a little bit more work since you'll need to find weekly readings (please do not scan and attach readings you have collecting dust in a file or in a cabinet unless they're REALLY useful). I do prefer to have text-book-free courses if I can since there's a lot of freedom with it and I know I can use current information while saving students money.

Instructional design suggestions:

Once you have a mess on your papers with course outcomes, weekly objectives, ideas about activities, assessments, and interactions, it's time to get your fingers moving on the keyboard within your course. Some institutions might require a navigation menu that cannot be changed. If that's true for you, I am sorry because it's not fun to be limited in that way. See what you have available to you and **only** use what is absolutely necessary on the navigation menu★. The more things to click, the more students will get confused. Typically you'll have:

- Announcements
- Syllabus
- Modules/Units/Lessons (all of the learning content is here)
- Discussions/Forums
- Tests/Assessments (use this ONLY if you cannot put the tests/quizzes within the modules/units/lessons area)
- Grades
- Email/Messages/Tools (a quick email or message tool to reach you or other students)

I suggest that you put all of your learning content in ONE area if you can. I will usually start off with the weekly objectives listed at the top. I've been known to theme each week too... not like Mardi Gras or puppies, but each week I will have the same language used with different content (I don't use all of these every week):

Introduction & Objectives:
What to Read:
What to Discuss:
What to Do:
Resources:

Here are some screen shots from a Modern British Literature class I designed. I didn't use these exact categories, but you get the general idea of organization. This is Blackboard, version 9, just so you know your LMS may not look like this. I do apologize if the images are difficult to read and the fact that the font is not consistent. That's what happens with screen shots, unfortunately.

Week 3 Objectives

- interpret and discuss the writings of Charles Dickens
- explain typical themes presented in the writings of Dickens
- apply literary analysis and interpretation skills to Dickens' works

Read

American Notes Understand that this is a LONG piece from Dickens. However, it's an important piece as it is journal-like reflection of his first trip to America and what he saw there. Just so you know, he was basically appalled at the way America was (slavery, tobacco chewing) and many Americans criticized him because of what he wrote.

The first link above is the link to the beginning of the work, but perhaps you can find enjoyable reading in some of the later chapters.
Boston chapter

New York chapter

Philadelphia chapter

Cincinnati chapter

Kentucky/Ohio chapter

Charles Dickens: The Battle of Life: A Love Story (Scroll down a bit to get to the story)

Discuss

Choose 2 discussion questions to answer. Make sure they are both posted separately. Respond to 3 classmates by Sunday.

DQ 1: Many scholars think that Charles Dickens believed that he had a moral responsibility as a writer, which is to instill moral behavior in his readers. Do you see any examples of this in anything we read this week? If so, do provide specific references and describe the moral behavior you believe he is trying to encourage.

DQ 2: Choose two of the chapters from Dickens' American Notes and compare and contrast his visits to these different locations. How were the descriptions similar? How were they different? Which place do you think he preferred between the two? How do you know?

DQ 3: Some people think that The Battle for Life: A Love Story is written as a metaphor for the general struggles of ordinary people with their lives. Do you agree with this? If so, provide evidence to support your position. If you disagree, what would you say it's representing?

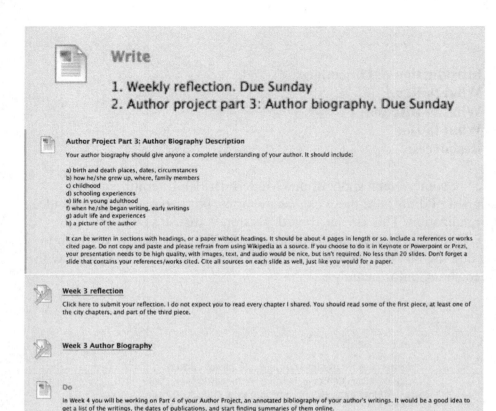

Write

1. Weekly reflection. Due Sunday
2. Author project part 3: Author biography. Due Sunday

Author Project Part 3: Author Biography Description

Your author biography should give anyone a complete understanding of your author. It should include:

a) birth and death places, dates, circumstances
b) how he/she grew up, where, family members
c) childhood
d) schooling experiences
e) life in young adulthood
f) when he/she began writing, early writings
g) adult life and experiences
h) a picture of the author

It can be written in sections with headings, or a paper without headings. It should be about 4 pages in length or so. Include a references or works cited page. Do not copy and paste and please refrain from using Wikipedia as a source. If you choose to do it in Keynote or Powerpoint or Prezi, your presentation needs to be high quality, with images, text, and audio would be nice, but isn't required. No less than 20 slides. Don't forget a slide that contains your references/works cited. Cite all sources on each slide as well, just like you would for a paper.

Week 3 reflection

Click here to submit your reflection. I do not expect you to read every chapter I shared. You should read some of the first piece, at least one of the city chapters, and part of the third piece.

Week 3 Author Biography

Do

In Week 4 you will be working on Part 4 of your Author Project, an annotated bibliography of your author's writings. It would be a good idea to get a list of the writings, the dates of publications, and start finding summaries of them online.

Each week I will change the color of each of those (just for aesthetics and because I dig color) and because they know what to expect, the consistency will help you design and help the students feel comfortable right away. It's entirely possible to even have three categories such as "Read, Discuss, Apply"★. It just depends on you and your own creativity and organizational preferences. I do like to see a sound organizational structure in online classes and not one specific way is the "right" way.

You should create content too:

Sound organization is just part of the 'quality' picture of course design. There are other important elements like what's contained in those course components. One thing that I see missing from online courses most of the time is the instructor-created content. Granted, the instructors do design the class, but I'm talking about the content that really shows what the instructor knows about the subject. There are usually no lectures in online courses, so there's no time for you to tell your students stories, or exemplify a concept. So, you have to make an effort to do this for your

24

online students. I like to call these 'instructor notes' or 'lecture notes"★. They don't have to be long, nor should they be because students will probably not read them if they're more than 2 pages long.

Each week, offer your own take on that week's learning through written instructor notes that are placed in your "Read" section. If you have the ability, you can also record an audio version or a podcast. However, do not depend on an audio or podcast only because that is not ADA compliant. Use them as supplements to a written document. These notes provide the students with your unique 'voice' and experiences (and if you tell stories, even better). Please, I beg you, DO NOT USE POWER POINT. That's a presentation tool, not a tool to use in this circumstance. I am not a hater on Power Point, although the faculty where I work might argue otherwise and have some significant evidence to support their claims, but… it's just that students who learn online are usually busy, do not want to waste time scrolling through 25 pages of outlined text that might not mean anything to them. If they want to take notes on the chapter and a PPT is provided, why not just write an outline in a Word document and save the students 22 pages of paper and ink?

Weekly learning units:

Start creating your weekly units in this order:

- Introduction & Weekly objectives
- Reading assignments & Videos (or other multimedia)
- Discussion questions
- Activities/assessments

Save the activities and assignments for the final pieces you add or create in each week/unit because they take the most work. Plus, you'll want your objectives ready and able to be moved/modified if necessary before you put the work into designing an assignment or assessment. If you need help creating the course-level outcomes and/or unit-level learning objectives, there's help out there on the Internet and perhaps within your institution as well. Read more about creating some of these items in the other chapters of this book.

Save directional content for last:

Don't forget that after you get your content designed, then it's time to develop your syllabus and course schedule. I would wait until you're about done to get that syllabus finalized because you might change your approaches once you have the bigger picture of the course★. Do avoid putting due dates on your syllabus unless you are required to★. Some institutions have very specific requirements about course syllabi, so start with your institutional requirements and ignore me if the two are not compatible.

I suggest having due dates in ONE location in your course and nowhere else★. That location is a course schedule. Why? Because once you design a course for the first time you will NOT want to have to change every due date the next time you teach it. If you have due dates all over the place, then you'll have to go on a hunt to find them all the next time. It's very time consuming. This way the only document you have to change each time is the course schedule. In addition, you don't need to constantly remind students what's due and when. They have the file; they have access to it every time they're online. It is not your job to remind them. The exception is the Canvas LMS. You will want to make sure all assignments have due dates when you create them because a calendar is filled out automatically for the students.

Within the course I always have an agenda★. That agenda is not usually something that can be printed because the students can print the course schedule. The agenda might appear on the outside of a learning unit, like you see below (this example is from Blackboard 9).

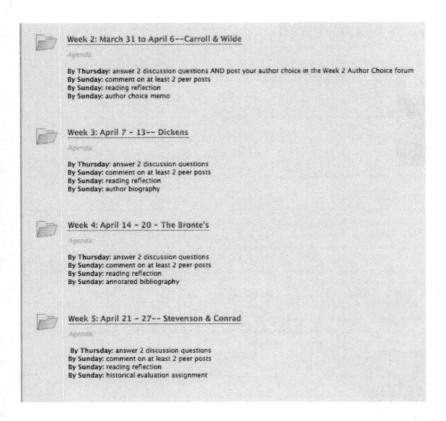

Week 2: March 31 to April 6--Carroll & Wilde

Agenda:

By Thursday: answer 2 discussion questions AND post your author choice in the Week 2 Author Choice forum
By Sunday: comment on at least 2 peer posts
By Sunday: reading reflection
By Sunday: author choice memo

Week 3: April 7 - 13-- Dickens

Agenda:

By Thursday: answer 2 discussion questions
By Sunday: comment on at least 2 peer posts
By Sunday: reading reflection
By Sunday: author biography

Week 4: April 14 - 20 - The Bronte's

Agenda:

By Thursday: answer 2 discussion questions
By Sunday: comment on at least 2 peer posts
By Sunday: reading reflection
By Sunday: annotated bibliography

Week 5: April 21 - 27-- Stevenson & Conrad

Agenda:

By Thursday: answer 2 discussion questions
By Sunday: comment on at least 2 peer posts
By Sunday: reading reflection
By Sunday: historical evaluation assignment

I used due DAYS, not dates★. The dates are on the course schedule that I change each semester.

The personalization factor:

One other important item to include is **YOU**. Yes, indeed, your students should have a place to go that tells them all about you. If your LMS does not provide you with an area like "Instructor" or "Faculty", then you can put it on your syllabus or in your introductions forum. I like to include a picture and suggest you do the same. Treat your online students the same way as you would your face-to-face students★. I've seen several instructors say 'no' to sharing their photo and one person said it was for privacy reasons, the other because he did not want the students to judge him from his appearance. Neither of them make much sense to me because unless they're teaching behind a curtain or a wall in a traditional class, why should the online students have to experience that lack of information? It doesn't seem fair that just because of the learning medium that they're not given the same privileges or experiences. On the next page is a sample of my instructor information (it was too big to fit here and it might be fuzzy to read and I'm sorry).

My name is Dr. Angela Velez-Solic and I will be instructing you this term!

Educationally speaking, I have my BA in English & Education, my MA in English, and my Ph.D. in Adult Education, with some emphasis in online learning.

I've been teaching at the college level since 1998 and I've loved it ever since. I started teaching online in 2005; at first I wasn't convinced it was right for me as a teacher, but I soon realized that I could be just as effective through the computer as I was in the face to face classroom! In 2007 I started working full time in faculty support, training and development, and had teaching as a part time gig. I remain that way now.

I work full time at Indiana University Northwest as Associate Director for the Center for Innovation & Scholarship in Teaching & Learning and Assistant Professor of Education. Yep, I live over in Indiana, not far from Chicago.
I really love my job. I do a lot of training for college faculty-- how to teach online and how to design online classes.

Personally speaking, I have a husband, Brian and 3 sons and a daughter-- Andrew, 17, Devin, 15, Zack, 12, and Julia, 10. I also have 3 step children, a boy who's 14 and twin girls who are 9. I absolutely love being outdoors, camping, hiking, fishing, and especially riding my Harley Davidson. I have a 2007 Low Rider.. it's the most wonderful type of freedom in the world. Here's a picture of it!

Besides that, I enjoy photography, writing poetry, and enjoying time with my kids.
My favorite place to be in the entire world is in Southwest Virginia (where Daniel Boone spent a lot of time).

By the way, you can call me Dr. Solic, Doc, or Angela, whatever makes you comfortable

Being a 'person' and not a machine is a big deal. Make sure your students know you and that you share as much of yourself as you feel comfortable sharing. Not everyone is as open as I am, nor do I expect everyone to be; however, being open, honest, real, and approachable happens to be part of the reason I am good at what I do.

Once you're finished with your syllabus, I challenge you to create a Week 0 or Week 1 quiz that covers important information from your syllabus★. You should ask them how many days a week they have to log in, how many posts they have to make, how many days a week they need to participate on the discussion forums, etc. Also include information about you too, if you want! This forces them to read the syllabus and know what's expected. Sometimes I make this worth 10 points (low value), and sometimes it's the only extra credit opportunity they get! I let them take it as many times as they want to earn full points too, but I only leave it open that first week.

For those of you who really want to know that your students are actually READING the material you assign them to read, there a few ways to make sure or try to make sure they do it★.

1. Assign reading reflection. I do this in my literature classes. I tell them they have to write questions, responses, gut reactions, whatever, to EACH assigned reading. I don't care if it's sentences, bullet points, or even mind maps. I want to see evidence of them reading a piece and thinking about it. I grade these quickly because I ask them to label each reading. I also don't allow them to attach them. I ask them to copy and paste into the assignment box so I get through them very quickly.

2. Make the discussion questions relate to the reading. I will talk more about this in another chapter. This one isn't as much insurance as #1 and #3.

3. Have a short quiz. I am not a big fan of these, but if you want to have something self-graded, create a short quiz on the reading, but please no lower- level (Bloom's Taxonomy) thinking questions.

All right, what are you waiting for? Get that paper out, get that pencil sharpened and get busy!

S. Campbell / Flickr

Chapter 4 Checklist: Getting started

- It is totally ok to feel freaked out, anxious, and uncertain
- Start off low-tech and plan with pencil and paper if you want
- You need to know the course-level learning outcomes first
- The course outcomes need to be broken down into weekly objectives
- Don't have more than 2 things to manually grade each week
- What you have your students doing needs to match with those objectives
- Keep the navigation menu simple. Less is more in terms of places to click
- Organize weekly content consistently. Choose clever categories
- You need to create content too. Include your voice and wisdom each week
- Power Points are not appropriate learning tools for online classes
- Put course due dates in ONE place in the course, such as on a schedule/calendar
- Use agendas for each week to keep students organized
- Treat your online students the same as your face-to-face students
- Create a syllabus quiz that covers policies and expectations

5

Make their time worth it

Off of the top of your head, right now, think about your most memorable learning experience in college. Who was teaching? How was he or she teaching? What were you *doing*? I wrote the word doing and put it in bold to make sure you paid attention to it. I would bet my bottom dollar that your memory did not involve someone talking to you, or of you reading a textbook chapter, but of you being *involved* in your learning by actively *doing* something with it.

For me, I remember Carol Winters from Grand Valley State University. She taught methods courses in reading and writing for elementary education majors. I remember her courses so well because we were always *doing.* I remember my Shakespeare professor who had us acting out scenes from plays so that they became real to us in a different way. I apologize for not remembering his name (I think it was Campbell), but I absolutely remember the impact of the course and that he was very tall, had long brown hair, always wore jeans and high top Converse. While these things happened in traditional courses, there's no excuse why you can't have your students *doing* as much as possible in online and hybrid courses.

Project, problem, and case-based activities:

My favorite activities for online courses are: project-based, problem-based, and case-based. I also believe (this is where the Adult Education Ph.D. shows its true colors) that learning in college should be transformative and involve the students in thinking about, reacting to, and doing things in their world in order to make it a better place to live. Let me see if I can give you some very specific examples that show you how I have accomplished these things in my own classes. The screen shot on the next page is from a Business Communication and Writing course.

The basics

Ok, so what's this project all about?

For this class you're going to be an owner of a quickly growing business in the US. You've made a decision to open another branch of your company overseas. This project will consist of different communications you will make to various people about your decision.

By the second week you need to figure out:
1. What's your business?
- give it a name
- have a product/process, etc.
- choose a city for your headquarters

2. Where are you going?
- choose from the list of places provided in the section below. These are FIRST COME FIRST TAKE. You have to visit the Week 2 forum: Country Choices and post your choice. If yours is already taken, choose another. No duplicates allowed.

Week 2: You will write a memo of intent to me, your instructor, as your audience. You will tell me your business, what you sell or do, where you're going, and why you're going there.

Week 4: This assignment will be a Proposal for Action that you will give to the employees of your company. You will be informing them of the newest branch of your company and attempt to get their support, and, hopefully, their willingness to work overseas.

Week 6: Now that the word is out, you will need to approach the media to quell rumors that your business is shutting down and you're just outsourcing to make a buck. Therefore, this week you will turn in a business letter to local media outlets. It should be publishable in a local newspaper.

Week 8: You're having a tough time convincing some of your prized employees to venture overseas to get the new branch going. So, you create a visually appealing, persuasively written brochure in an attempt to get more interest and support from your employees.

Week 11: Now that you've gathered enough employees, you need to adequately prepare them for the culture in which they will live and work for many months. This assignment will be a research report (a handbook for your employees) about the verbal and nonverbal communication expectations in your country, typical business practices, and other cultural anomalies that might affect their work lives.

Week 14: The time has come to make a presentation to the entire company about your plans, data that prove why this was a good idea, who is going, what they will be doing over there, for how long, and the general outlook of this venture for the company's future.

I've taken the typical types of business writing pieces and broken them down into small assignments as part of a bigger course project that is realistic, meaningful, and practical. My students are pretending to be business owners and they will make up their company's name, product or service, and choose a country from my list of countries where they will open a new branch of their business. What they come up with is nothing short of spectacular!

The students have freedom to be creative; trust me, they rise to the occasion! One student was opening a 10,000 square foot "Video game Coliseum" in South Korea, another an Organic Produce distributor in Germany. One of my all-time favorites was a wine tasting 'pub crawl' type of business opening in the Loire Valley of France! I mix the project parts with short, low-stakes quizzes every other week based upon the very expensive book they had to purchase, just to make sure they are reading and responsible for the textbook learning as well as weekly discussions and three peer reviews.

In another course, which is a freshman-type of academic strategies classes, I have the students come up with a social issue in their local area that they want to see change. It could be child abuse awareness, the homeless, domestic violence awareness, pollution, saving an historic building, or anything that they care about. During the course they will learn how to set goals, research social movements, write materials to  gather support (persuasive writing), read about people who almost never get media attention, but who have changed the world in some fantastic way, and get started on improving their cause. Each assignment builds upon the next and they learn key academic, writing, interpersonal, and intrapersonal skills along the way while also gaining confidence in themselves.

In my British Literature course I have them become an expert on an author. The entire accelerated 8-week course centers around this project. I give the students a lot of flexibility in terms of HOW the present the information. I accept all types of presentations, but have a common grading rubric that's general enough to work for anything. Their minds and technical abilities are the limit to what they can give me to show they've learned. On the following page is a screen shot of this course project.

The basics

Ok, so what's this project all about?

You'll be doing an in-depth author examination over the entire term. Here's a quick overview of what you will do each week.

Week 2: Part 1: You will choose a British writer and write me a memo about which author you're choosing and why you chose that particular author. Remember, no one can choose the same author. Therefore, be careful to watch the discussion forum called "Author Choices" so that you don't choose someone that has been chosen already. The list of authors is a little bit below this area.

Week 3: Part 2: At the end of this week you will turn in an author biography. This is research based, which means that you cannot just copy and paste the Wikipedia article on your author and pass that off as your paper. That's not going to work for me. Instead, you'll peruse the internet or other sources and find information about the author. You will be required to utilize EITHER MLA or APA style of formatting. If you don't know how to cite, I will provide you with some samples in this area. Just scroll down some.

Week 4: Part 3: This week you will work on an annotated bibliography of this author's works. So, again, you'll spend time research what this author wrote, when he or she wrote it, and what that piece is about. This bibliography can be presented in any way you choose, but what it must have is the book/poem/essay's title, date of publication, and a short summary of the piece (probably 100 words or so for each piece). These summaries must be in your own words. If you research these summaries, you need to provide proper citations.

Week 5: Part 4: This week you'll turn in an evaluation of the historical time period in which your author wrote. This might be similar to your timeline that you turned in during the first week, or it might be different. Generally, this is an overview of what was going on during the time that your author was publishing. This will be a paper, approximately 2 or 3 pages long. Again, use appropriate documentation. You can include images if you wish, but be sure they are properly cited. Images cannot be used to fill the page requirement.

Week 6: Part 5: This week's assignment is an comparison/contrast paper based on two of your author's written pieces. Ideally, you should choose two different pieces so that the comparison/contrast is easier on you. What I mean is if the author has a really 'dark' piece, and one that is perhaps uplifting and optimistic, that would be a good pair to compare/contrast. This should be a 3 to 4 page paper with appropriate documentation.

Week 7: This week you should work on compiling your final project. It should contain all of the pieces you wrote previously, with all documents revised and edited based upon the feedback you received on them. You should also have a title page, table of contents, and one page learning reflection.

Week 8: The final project will be turned in. You will peer review each other's projects this week as well.

This might seem way off topic, but when it comes time for you to decide on a new phone or car, does it make you happy that you can choose one of many different models? You will probably choose a model of car or phone that just looks, well, like something you would pick out, right? Choice is a good thing and it's also a good idea, when you can, to offer your students choices. I offer them choices in discussion questions (more on that in the next chapter) and sometimes choices in how they do some of their assignments like I just explained with the British Lit class. As long as they know what they have to cover, and how you're going to grade them, it's safe to give them options.

I have had so many student comments about this on my evaluations—not just that I give them choices and there's a sense of freedom they get from it, but also from having practical and fun assignments. Having choices gives them freedom to do what they enjoy and share information how they'd like to share it, and it also makes grading really interesting because I never know what I'm going to open next! Grading is one of the most annoying and time-consuming parts of our jobs, isn't it? Speaking of that...

What happens with all of these courses is that I grade progressively, so in the end, when they bring it all together, not much is a surprise to me and they also had time to revise assignments that needed some help. They had time to even add something if they missed an assignment (which doesn't usually happen) for their final piece. This makes end-of-term grading a lot less stressful for me, and for them! What's even better is these students truly remember these learning experiences and I can say that because my students do keep in touch with me well after they leave my classes.

I know that these are very humanities-based, undergraduate projects and courses. Sorry, I can't help it. It is my hope that I will be designing some graduate courses in education at some point in the future and once I do, I will provide those examples. When you teach graduate courses I think you have even more freedom to put the students to work on projects, especially ones that can affect their work or life environments. Of course, graduate students still need to learn how to research and disseminate findings as well as effectively communicate their research in writing, but that can still happen even if the course has practical, engaging assignments. Maybe they can focus on a problem in their workplace, research a subject that directly affects them, or create something that benefits those in their work or local community. Give it some thought.

Challenge yourself if you're in business, the sciences, or even accounting! I was sent an email from a faculty member who is on The Teaching Professor's listserv. Within that particular message was information about a man by the name of Gleb Tsipursky of The Ohio State University. In the National Teaching & Learning Forum Newsletter (http://ntlf.com/about.aspx) from February of 2014 was a neat idea called "Class-Sourcing" ★. Instead of writing long research papers to prove what they learn, this innovative thinker had his students create digital repositories of artifacts on topics they chose relating to his course (which is in history, but this can be used for any subject). They made websites or Pinterest boards and other things. Check out his site to learn more: http://www.glebtsipursky.com/teaching/classsourcing.

The reality is that these students need to situate their learning within the real world in which they are living now and the very different world in which they will live and work once they graduate. They need to know how to use the Internet to do quality research; they need to know how to use the digital tools available to them. They can leave their college with all kinds of theoretical knowledge, but is that going to help them complete a project on time, figure out how to use technology to support their efforts, or solve a complex problem that needed to be solved yesterday? I hear stories from my engineer husband of people who are hired with advanced degrees in engineering, but who can't seem to handle a difficult problem with a valve that doesn't work or a design that needs to be scaled differently at the last minute. He said that these people couldn't turn to a textbook for an answer; they need to have learned some skills through practice, failure, and problem solving.

Providing students with problems to solve (such as, for example, a homeless issue in St. Louis, Missouri) and giving them the tools they need to investigate, analyze, read, synthesize, suppose, create, and evaluate will result in amazing learning experiences which will spill over into other parts of their lives.

M. Krzeszak / Flickr

You're not just teaching them psychology, sociology, biology, criminology, history, or international finance, you're teaching them **how to be** someone who can interact within the context of a new environment with new problems. Students who do too much reading and recitation do not learn how to interact within new environments. They learn basic knowledge, if it even sticks in their heads after the exams. I am not saying it's bad to learn facts, formulas, or theories. I am saying it's bad to learn them without application.

Case studies are great ways to learn facts and then put students in situations where they need to apply that knowledge. I cannot think of a single subject in which case studies cannot be used. You can provide them yourself, or if you're teaching a higher-level undergrad or graduate level course, challenge the students to create their own in groups or individually. Then they can exchange case studies and come up with responses for an assignment. I think it's particularly wonderful to gather case studies from real practitioners in a field. How great is it to tell students, "This really happened... what would you do?"

Problem-based learning can be just as engaging. You can present the students with a problem and have them figure out how they would solve it. Just like case studies, you can have students write their own problems, exchange them, and attempt to solve the problems. Students are treasure troves of knowledge and experiences, especially in online courses where most of the students are adults with jobs, families, and work experience. Tap into those experiences and that life wisdom! When students can share situations from their own lives, it links living to learning and makes it personal, transformational, and unforgettable!

Let me give you a fantastic example of 'doing'. A social work professor at Northeastern Illinois University, Jane Peller, took a little Flip Video Camera (this was before most digital cameras also had HD video built in) and stopped people at her gym. She gave them a little script and said, "Act like you're a grieving widow who lost her husband of 50 years." Then she would ask them questions and ask them to react in character. She used these little clips as case studies and her gym-colleagues-turned-actors were happy to help. She was able to upload the video clips into a private YouTube account so her online students could easily access them through the LMS (I am sure you remember that term by now). She then put the video links into Lectora or Snap! (content authoring tools) so that when the students played them, they would have to choose the appropriate response (as a therapist) to specific clips of the video. They learned, through practice, how to respond to clients in a counseling situation. The impact on the students was almost priceless.

What about speeches, presentations, and language learners?

Many institutions require students to complete speeches or presentations as part of the curriculum. I have had many discussions with people from many different institutions about how it's possible to take a public speaking class online and not defeat the purpose of the course. Some faculty who teach communication courses can't get past the face-to-face speech and refuse to consider anything but to prove the students have learned the material or to confidently assess the student's ability to give a speech. I think the word "public" makes it sticky. If the course were just "Speech and Presentation", then we wouldn't have such a problem, would we?

O. Hotshot / Flickr

I'm not a communication professor, so my views are skewed about whether the students must present in a public environment. I've taught speech, though, but only face-to-face. I have taught online courses that had required presentations or speeches and the way both institutions enforced the requirement without requiring synchronous meetings was by using software paid for by the university.

One was called YouSeeU and students record their presentations through that software. I watch their presentations/speeches and grade them★. Another possibility is called Present.me. I can assure you that my students were just as nervous recording as they would have been standing in front of people in a room. In addition, as technology keeps moving forward, students will need to learn how to communicate electronically. They will experience virtual meetings and virtual presentations and those may become more common than a traditional, sitting-in-front-of-you audience. Thus, they need to get used to that way of communicating too. The image above is from Second Life, a virtual world that can enhance online learning experiences.

If your course usually involves synchronous speeches, consider making them asynchronous. There are many programs available to allow this to happen. Some LMSs even have built-in recording software so you and your students don't need to go anywhere to record a presentation! If you don't, and require synchronous time with your online students, you must at least inform them before the course begins about which days and times they will be required to be at a specific place at a specific time (even if it's online in a program like Adobe Connect). What I've seen happen is the faculty members who **do not** require synchronous meetings will have higher student enrollment than those who do. It might not be right, but it is reality. The virtual speeches and presentations are just another way of getting the students active and 'doing'!

I do not believe for one minute that there's any subject that cannot be taught online. Technology is advanced enough that we can see and

38

hear each other with relative ease even through cyber-space. For students learning a foreign language, the LMS might have built-in audio tools. I know that at the time of this writing the only mainstream LMS that does is Canvas. However, that does not mean online language instruction is doomed. If you are allowed to, please consider using audio recording tools like Soundcloud, the webcam recording feature in YouTube, or the tool Voicethread, which requires a license. These are fantastic tools that will allow you, the instructor, to offer voice prompts and give your students a way to respond to you and their classmates using the language. Instead of having students take a paper test, require them to respond to a question you pose in Spanish using a webcam. Have them submit the video link as their assignment. These are just a few possibilities.

The moral of this section is that you should want your students walking away from your classroom (or logging off for the last time) thinking, "Wow, that was amazing. I not only learned about _____, but I will always remember how this course changed my life." That doesn't happen when students are stuck reading a textbook, answering boring discussion questions and taking exams. If you struggle with how to re-create your course into one that is meaningful, practical, and active, seek someone out to help you! There's nothing wrong with that. Sometimes people can really be very black and white in their minds and stuck in a rut of 'one right way' of teaching a subject when you just need someone who can think in many shades of grey to help you see your way out.

Chapter 5 checklist: Activities and Engagement

- o   Having students actively DOING is key to great learning!
- o   Give students choices in terms of how to present their knowledge
- o   Situated learning is beneficial. Make it part of their world
- o   It's bad to learn facts without application
- o   Tap into the student's experience to create case studies and problems for them to solve relevant to the learning
- o   Try to find creative ways of making learning moments relevant and real
- o   Speech classes can use tools like Adobe Connect or YouSeeU to simulate the speech environment
- o   Languages can be taught online. Utilize audio and video tools to record prompts and require recorded responses

6

Let's give 'em something to talk about

Interaction is the heart of an online course. I don't care if you're teaching them statistical analysis, biochemistry, or political science. There is always something to talk about. If I had a dollar for every instructor who told me, "My students work out problems. We don't have anything to

D. Shankbone / Flickr

discuss" I would be a really wealthy woman and I'd be driving that Dodge Challenger Hellcat by now.

I'm not, by the way. Moving on.

What I tell those people is: yes, you can discuss things even in a class that is filled with numeric formulas and logical problem solving. Of course, the discussion might not be as significant as it would be in a communication or education class, but it needs to be a part of the course. Including interactivity in skill-based classes takes some creativity, but it can be done.

Interaction is vital:

An active online course can be really intimidating to faculty members who aren't used to it. In a normal online course you *should* have interaction every week. Your students WILL talk and it can get really overwhelming if you have a big class. So, I will give you some tips and tricks in this chapter to manage discussions. What I want you to remember above all else, though, is that just because it's overwhelming, and just because it's busy does not mean that you should stay out of your student's discussions. No way. I'm not saying you need to be involved in discussions every single day (you should comply with your school's requirement if one exists), but you should be involved a few days a week. There are ways to be involved that will not take up an entire day or even more than about 30 minutes each time you decide to participate. I will explore this a little later in this chapter.

Discussion question techniques:

If you're teaching a freshman-level undergraduate class, consider having one discussion question a week. However, provide them with at least two questions or even three and let them choose which discussion question they'd like to answer★. Yes, I know this means you have to take more time to write those questions, but it will be worth it in the end. If you're teaching junior-level through graduate students, two discussion questions a week is fine. Again, give them at least one more question than you require so they can choose which ones to answer. I have required two in a sophomore level literature course only because it was an accelerated 8-week format. If it were 16 weeks I would have required one per week.

The first discussion question you should provide is an introduction. If the class opens a few days or a week before the course actually begins it will give the students a chance to start interacting early. You can ask them to share whatever personal information they're comfortable sharing, a picture if they know how, and even play icebreaker games! I have found much success with them as a matter of fact. My favorite is called "two truths and a lie". I tell the students, after their introduction, to share three statements, two of them should be true and one is not (or you can do two lies and a truth)★. Students should guess the lie (or the truth if you do the other game). The game keeps them wondering and it's even more fun when you play too. I tell them to come clean on the final day of the first week. There are many different icebreakers-- you can Google some other examples.

Besides the introduction forum, writing the other week's discussion questions is an art. It is not easy and does not just come naturally to most people. After all, you're used to asking questions in front of a class, getting responses (sometimes, or blank faces, or images of people texting and Facebooking), and going from there. It's all so…well, spontaneous. You don't have that space in time when discussion is happening in an online course. What you do have (and I will argue that it's way better), is an open room in which people are coming and going, talking, leaving, coming back, all hours of the day and night and leaving their words behind. You give up the non-verbal cues and spontaneity for constant discussion that goes places you will never imagine, as long as the questions are written well.

Before I give you a great formula for quality discussion questions, let me give you a list of a few things your discussion questions should NOT be. A poorly designed discussion prompt is a question:

- That can be answered with a yes or a no
- That has one or two correct answers
- That does not involve them reading the assigned readings/chapters
- Other people can easily modify and make it their own answer
- That doesn't relate to the week's learning objectives

Asking the students to define something.... um, no. What will happen? The first student who is really on the ball who posts early will write a fantastic answer and the other students will read it first, and give the same response. That is not discussing. That's boring and not even worth doing. Even if your LMS allows you to limit the student's ability to see other posts before he posts his own, the question is still not designed to elicit anything to really discuss.

Sometimes discussion questions don't have to be questions at all. One strategy shared by Maryellen Weimer in a Faculty Focus article is called "Save the last word for me". Students are grouped in halves (this will work best in a class of less than 30) and one half is asked to find a quote, theory, idea, or concept (you get the idea) from the reading or lesson that they would like to understand better. The other half of the students help explain the items posted. It can switch off too. I highly suggest visiting FacultyFocus.com and using their "Browse Topics" link at the top to find articles about discussions. They're brilliantly useful and quick to read.

One formula:

I like discussion questions that have two or three parts. They should involve the week's reading, should involve application of knowledge learned, and provide students with an opportunity to give a personal opinion or experience★. I am not saying that only questions that follow that prescription are 'good' questions. There are numerous ways to write

A. Jensen / Flickr

them, this is just one formula. Providing an opportunity to write about the reading gives them motivation to actually read and know what they're writing about or else look stupid; secondly, asking them to apply that new learning to a situation helps them put the learning into a realistic context; finally, providing a chance to share personal opinions or experiences will ensure that each answer WILL be different and more interesting to read than 25 of the same answers over and over again.

Discussion question examples:

When I train my faculty members I always teach them how to write discussion questions and have them practice by writing some. I will find you some examples from various disciplines. Please keep in mind that almost all of these are written by people who have not yet taught online. These questions may not all be the 'best', but they're pretty good if you ask me.

Example 1 (Nursing): *Many authors define Evidenced Based Practice (EBP). One of the best definitions and rationale for EBP comes from Boswell and Cannon (2007). They state, "EBP is defined as a research-based, decision-making process used to guide the delivery of holistic patient care by nurses. Holistic nursing care encompasses the clinical expertise of the nurse, patient preferences, cultural aspects, psychosocial facets, and biological components. The research process and scientific data generated serve as the foundation on which the decision-making process for nursing care is based. All nurses have the responsibility of ensuring that the care they provide to their clients is based on sound nursing knowledge, not just "the way we have always done it."*

Reflect on your clinical experiences to date and, in a few sentences, consider and discuss a practice you routinely do that might fall into the category of "the way we have always done it." For example, is turn q 2 hours based on any sound evidence, or is it just something we have always done?

Example 2 (History):

Consider Woodrow Wilson's 14 Points. Please answer each part of the question.
a) What were his main goals?
b) How realistic were these goals?
c) Was this a major shift for American foreign policy?
d) What about this era do you think caused that shift?
e) Are there any lasting impacts from Wilson's policies today?

Example 3 (Marketing):
*One of the outcomes of a successful marketing campaign is to influence what people **want** or perceive they need. Discuss why this is or is not ethical. Defend your position with examples of real-world consequences and benefits.*

Coke and Pepsi have been in heated competition for years. Compare the websites for Coke (www.coca-cola.com) and Pepsi (www.pepsi.com). Provide a marketing rationale for the significant differences that exist between the websites of the two companies.

Example 4 (Public Health):
Choose a federal public health agency and visit its website. Identify an issue it is currently addressing and the reasons for concern to the public. Discuss controversies that may be involved in actions the agency may have taken or need to take to address the issue.

Example 5 (Education):
In the book, *Huck's Raft*, Steven Mintz seeks to use historical evidence to refute and challenge prevailing myths about childhood and children's experience in American culture.

In Chapter [insert # & title] against which myth is Steven Mintz directing the bulk of his explanatory and descriptive efforts? In your response, include at least 4 "pieces of evidence" to support your myth-selection. One piece of evidence should be identified clearly as the "telling fact" that best establishes your argument.

Example 6 (Communication):
In Chuck Kleinhans' "Audio documentary: a polemical introduction for the visual studies crowd," he gives several examples pointing to the reason

44

for the continued relevance and success of audio documentary. For this discussion, listen and respond to one of the more successful audio documentary pieces created in this area: Ghetto 101

http://www.soundportraits.org/on-air/ghetto_life_101/audio.php

1. How do the documentarians construct a sense of space and place? Give concrete examples and make sure to note at what time in the production we can hear your examples.

2. Using this piece as inspiration, how would you go about creating in audio form a sense of space for your work?

Example 7 (Educational Psychology):
Piaget discusses the cognitive stages that people pass through and how they adapt their thinking. Do you agree or disagree with his theory? Give some personal examples or observations that support or refute his ideas.

Example 8 (Communication):
In the three video clips from "Crash" (2004), what are the three major ways the main characters demonstrated the concept SELF. Thoroughly analyze just one of the scenes, not all three. Refer to the text "self" in interpersonal communication--self-concept, self-awareness, and self-esteem. What particular behaviors were exhibited in the scene you selected and provide reasons for your answer. Lastly, reflect back to your self-introductions. Analyze your self-introduction, based on the chapter's readings.

Example 9 (Social Work):*In this era of immigration reform, what cultural areas of concern should a social worker be mindful of when evaluating depression when working with clients with ethnic backgrounds different than their own? What multi-generational issues should be explored?*

Example 10 (Geology):
In Michigan's Upper Peninsula, there are several rock exposures of 2.6 **billion** *year old pillow basalts. These are located along Hwy. 41, just west of the town of Marquette and are commonly visited by Earth Science students here and from students all over the Midwest. These pillow basalts are so old that they have lost their glassy appearance but maintain their*

telltale "pillow" shapes.

What interpretations can you make about the geologic environment 2.6 billion years ago in Michigan's Upper Peninsula?

Example 11 (Statistics):
This morning, in a daily column of Post-tribune, an article "Mother nature decides sex of baby" drew my attention. In it a reader states: "I'd like to have three children, and the odds are that at least one of them would be a little girl." Dr. Wallace, the owner of the column responds: "If indeed you were rewarded with three children, odds are about 88 percent that one of them would be a daughter." I wanted to write to Dr. Wallace and explain that odds are quotients of probabilities. The probability that one of the three children would be a daughter is 87.5% and odds in favor of having at least one daughter are 875 to 125 or 7 to 1. Do you think I should?
Find an article that misuses concepts of probability and/or miscalculates them. Explain in details what those mistakes were. Which corrections would you send to the editor of the newspaper or magazine to help him/her understand the errors made?

Example 12 (Finance):
Your text notes there are two major opinions as to the appropriate overall goal for the firm. One view claims the firm should strive to maximize shareholder wealth. The alternative view, the stakeholder capitalism model urges management to create value for all its stakeholders (stockholders, labor, the community, suppliers and so on). Which type of company would you rather work for after you graduate? Explain why.

I know I gave you a long list of them, but I want you to see how different they all are, but they're still good questions to get them really involved! I could go on and on, but I just went into one of my training courses and grabbed 12 of them and am glad they offer you some variety.

I was at a conference in 2012 and this woman who taught upper level education courses did some pretty spectacular things. She actually had her students self-evaluate their discussion activity during the course AND she had this neat requirement. Only the first 2 or 3 students were allowed to answer the weekly discussion question. Why? Well, each student was required to end his or her answer with a question related to that week's learning. The students who posted later had to answer one of the student-posed questions, which were sometimes more challenging to answer! They also had to end their posts with questions, even if they're the last person posting. That pushes them to think even deeper about the subject matter! There's motivation for students to post early in this situation because later posters will have a harder time coming up with a question that hasn't already been asked! That's just genius.

Planning and managing discussions:

Planning and managing discussions is not easy. In smaller classes discussions can lag a little bit, so you might need to be watchful and encouraging to your students to get in there and post. If your class has more than 20 or 25 students, it can get really, really busy. Visit chapter 10 to get some advice about larger courses.

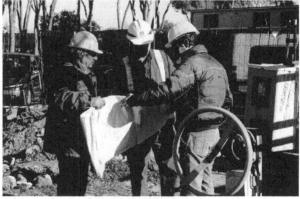

Being able to manage discussions is a skill that you will learn over time, but one of the reasons you have this book is to save that time

US Army Corps of Engineers / Flickr

of having to learn things the hard way, right? I know you're smart like that. When it comes to having students post in discussion, the first hard lesson learned is that you need to be crystal clear about what you expect. I mean completely lucid. Leave nothing to guess, and no loopholes to find. In your syllabus you need to have directions about discussions that tell them★:

- How many questions to answer each week

- How often they need to log in and participate in the weekly forum (2, 3, or 4 days a week with 3 days a week being average)

- How many posts they need to make each week (average is 2 or three quality peer replies per week in addition to the discussion question reply/replies)

- What a 'quality' post looks like for a discussion question reply (how many words, on average? Should they include citations? Citations are recommended, of course, for graduate courses)

- What a quality peer response looks like (again, how many words on average?) with a few examples of good and bad posts

I will provide them with examples of peer replies just so they can visualize what I am suggesting because students might not understand what 50 or 100 words 'looks' like nor what really contributing to a discussion looks like (and it's not saying, "Wow, what a great post. Good job!"). Essentially, give your students some suggestions for how to participate. Besides what you see above, think about the following★:

- If you agree with someone's post or like what they said, then explain why you agree. Be specific. Give details. Don't stop with this statement- follow up with anything else you thought of while reading the post

- Connect the student's post with something else relevant— another student's post, a previous topic covered in class, a current event, or ask the student how what they posted relates to something else

- Challenge the student to a hypothetical situation. Do the "what if…." "Then what" tactic. What if x happened instead? Then what would the reaction be? Or Then what would you do? Or, then what would you suggest?

- Ask the student an open ended question like, what do you think might happen (pick a time frame or situation)? Or, why is this issue so important to you?

- Ask the student for more evidence to support her post. Many times students say things without proper support for their opinions or assertions. Call them out on in (nicely) and ask for evidence. You might even go so far as to provide evidence to the CONTRARY of what the student wrote—in that situation, ask the student to respond to your evidence

Grading discussions:

Discussion should be a decent part of the course grade. An average percentage is about 20%. Students will need to know the criteria on which you're grading them every week, so create a discussion rubric or at least provide them with criteria that are easy to find and refer to. Some LMSs have the ability for you to use a rubric while grading (so you just click the categories), while many do not. Often I just provide points and some feedback.

Grading and giving feedback on discussion can be a very time consuming task. I will not lie to you and say that it isn't. There are strategies to decrease the time you spend grading, though. Here are mine, again, learned the hard way because no one taught me how to do these things.

- Make sure you have a folder on your computer for every course you teach online first.

- Create a document called "COM 220 Discussion Feedback" (but, of course, your course name might be different). On that document you will save feedback responses for each week. So, the first week you grade, first open that document and create three levels of feedback.

- Write feedback for: exceeds expectations, meets expectations, and needs improvement.

- Make sure your student posts and peer replies are all in ONE forum each week

- I usually create the same exact start, no matter which level it is and those sentences relate to that week's discussion★. Here is an example of three levels of feedback for a course:

Exceeds:
[Student name], learning about business proposals is something that is necessary if you ever find yourself involved

49

in a business. I hope that you were able to read several examples to see different perspectives and types of proposals—at least you know what NOT to do! I am very pleased with your performance in the forum, from your initial post through the many peer responses. You are an excellent model for the other students!

Meets:

[Student name], learning about business proposals is something that is necessary if you ever find yourself involved in a business. I hope that you were able to read several examples to see different perspectives and types of proposals—at least you know what NOT to do! You successfully met the requirements of discussion this week— have a great week 5!

Needs Improvement:

[Student name], learning about business proposals is something that is necessary if you ever find yourself involved in a business. I hope that you were able to read several examples to see different perspectives and types of proposals—at least you know what NOT to do! Your participation this week did not meet the minimum requirements. I'd like to see you earn full credit next week, so be sure and re-review those requirements outlined in the syllabus.

What ends up happening is when it's time to grade I keep these handy. Almost always my students' performance fits into one of these three categories. After the first few weeks I will usually say "in order to get full credit please refer to the syllabus. I look forward to your participation next week". Once I give my students points, I copy and paste the feedback from my file. I always include the student's first name before I paste and once in a while I will need to modify, but not normally.

Being part of the interaction:

Besides starting, managing, monitoring, and grading, you still have more to do when it comes to discussions. I know, I know, that seems like a lot of work, doesn't it? What more could you possibly need to do?

Participate.

There's room for you in your class discussions and if you're not there, your lack of presence will certainly be noticed and missed. There are many instructors who do not believe that they should participate in online class discussions. I often wonder why. It could be that it does take time and they are already busy enough and don't want to take that time. It might even be that they think that their presence would negatively affect student-to-student interaction. I've heard these and other reasons, but I feel strongly enough about the importance of you participating that I dismiss them all and encourage all faculty I train to have a role in what's being said each week.

s.h.u.t.t.e.r.b.u.g / Flickr

Did you know that most of the for-profits and some private institutions demand that their instructors participate on a certain number of days per week? Some even prescribe the number of posts per week. They watch, too. That's because they know that active faculty make for happy students. I am not condoning this practice, by the way, just giving you the head's up that it does exist.

I don't think that you have to be in the discussions every day. I'm not saying that you have to post all of the time, either. I am just saying that you need to have a presence. How you do that could vary, but I can give you some hints to decrease the amount of time it would take, but still ensure your students feel supported, like you are an active participant in their learning. I will tend to participate a few days a week in discussions with the exception of the first week's introduction forum. I am there every day and respond to every introductory post. I suggest you do the same as long as your class is a reasonable size (less than 30). It's a wonderful move in the right direction to give each student a personal 'hello' and welcome.

One way is to set a schedule of which days you will participate★. If your week starts on Monday, and you request that their initial discussion posts are due on Wednesday, you might schedule your own participation on Thursday and Saturday (this is my typical schedule). I usually use Tuesday and Wednesday as grading days unless I have papers to grade and in that case it takes most of the week to get through papers. Mondays I relax and only check for questions and make sure my announcements posted and all content is viewable by the students. If you schedule your days, be sure to put it on a calendar and/or set a phone reminder so you stick to it.

Another idea to save time is to open a Word File and shrink it so it takes up half of your screen. Then, open up your discussion forum and shrink that window to take up the other half. If you're super cool and have two screens, then you embrace that awesomeness and have the file on one screen and the forum on the other. Click on a discussion question and open all of the posts so you can scroll through them. As you read, take note of interesting things the students say, questions that you think of, or anything else. Type them on the Word file★. Use student names, too. I put them in bold or highlight them.

Once you are through, make sure to mark all of the posts as 'read'. Then, look to see what you have on your Word file. I usually separate them into posts. I will create a new thread and make my subject line creative, especially something like, "Please read..." Sometimes I will even put individual student names in the subject line. It's much better to have a post from you as its own thread instead of responding to a student post, which might only get read by one or two students because it's lost in a maze of other posts★.

A final idea is to keep a file of discussion replies that are not focused on student posts★. They could be little snippets of experience from you, words of wisdom, etc. that relate to that week's discussion question. You can use these as posts during the week's discussion and reuse them each time you teach the class. Make sure and update that file as often as you can. If you happen to think of something while you're teaching, put a copy of that post in your file. It really helps, especially those times when life and work runs away with you and you suddenly realize it's Friday and you haven't been in the discussions at all that week (but, of course, **I** have never done such a thing). I'm lying, because of course I have, but I feel bad when I do that.

I know that this discussion forum stuff can get monotonous, but it's up to you to make it fun and exciting! The questions are the bulk of the responsibility-- get those done well and you're good to go. There are also some tools out there to make it less monotonous. For example, I absolutely love Voicethread. It used to be free, now there's just a simple version that's free, but to really get the quality interaction you'll need a license. What happens is you can embed a Voicethread within a discussion forum and students, once they have accounts, can make video and/or audio replies. Then, you click on the student's picture or avatar to hear, watch, or read what they have to say. Way cool. Plus, you can put your question in the middle of the voice thread or a video. Check it out.

Chapter 6 checklist: Interaction

- o   Interaction is the heart of an online course
- o   Provide them with one more question than you require them to answer to give them a choice of which questions to answer
- o   You have to tell him how often to participate: number, how many days, how many peer replies
- o   Require a discussion response mid week and allow discussion to keep going until the final day of the week. Don't cut it off before the weekend!
- o   Give students some examples of how best to interact in discussions
- o   Write 3 levels of discussion feedback and save them to copy/paste for feedback (if allowed by your institution)
- o   Instead of replying to individuals, make group comments using individual names
- o   Have a file of "go to" discussion posts that are not focused on student replies, but on content for busy times
- o   Voicethread is a good way to decrease the monotony of discussion forums
- o   Visit facultyfocus.com and use "browse topics" to find more tips about discussion techniques

7

Assessment is a four-letter word

I am definitely not going to sit here and tell you that I am an expert at assessment. Not even close. I don't claim to know it all; I don't even claim to know a lot about it. What I do know is that my students do learn and I know how I measure that. However, how students learn definitely depends on a lot of factors, including the subject, the instructor, and how that learning is presented to the student. *If* the students learn, and *to what extent* they learn is something that all institutions seek to understand, measure, and quantify since accreditation and money tend to relate to those measurements.

Start with objectives:

Pippalou / Morguefile

My first piece of advice is: don't create your assessments until you've written your course outcomes and unit objectives★. Why? You're putting the cart before the horse. Unless he's a quality, trained jumper, he might not know to jump over that cart and get in front. I will repeat just for emphasis and dramatics: **Start with your outcomes and objectives first.** Then, evaluate how you plan to assess your students.

If you are using a traditional test to assess, read through it. Look at your unit objectives and your course outcomes. Does that test measure them? It should not be measuring something that is not stated in your objectives. Many times I have seen faculty members grab test questions from a publisher's test pool only to be testing on items that were never assigned in the book, or items that had nothing to do with the objectives. That is not good form.

Traditional testing:

I have to make a quick qualification here. I am honest to a fault and I apologize if that offends my test-loving peers. I don't like tests, especially the traditional ones that ask me to fill in a bubble or circle the ONE right answer. I've never tested well, and I probably never will. As a teenager I was judged on my standardized test scores that didn't allow me entrance in the college I wanted to attend. Fortunately, the tests did not accurately measure my ability to be a very good student and earn high grades throughout my degrees. Thus, my direct experience affects how I view traditional examinations.

As an educator, though (I'm not a technologist... I am an educator and have been for my entire life and career) the fact that a student can take a test well doesn't really tell me much. Grant Wiggins agrees with me too. Don't know who he is? Google him. When someone tests well, it could be because:

- That the student is very good at memorizing information.

- That the student doesn't over-analyze every question to death and despite understanding the information, he is unable to prove it because he confuses himself because he things it 'could' be A, and it's possibly B, definitely not C or D, though.

- That the student crammed right before the exam and everything is fresh in her mind, but if asked to apply the information she will stare at you like a deer in headlights.

Ok, I know that's not very fair. Students can show that they've learned *something* from exams and I know that doctors, nurses, and other medical professionals must take exams to prove they learn the information. However, they must also prove that they can apply that information during many hours of clinical work and rotations.

My oldest son is a fantastic test taker. He was fortunate enough to have his father's right brain and my left brain. He has verbal and mathematical intelligence, so he thinks logically and creatively. He scores insanely high on standardized tests. Does that mean he will succeed in college? Probably not. It takes more than the ability to test well to get through college with a good GPA. My son, though, at 17, feels very secure that college might not be so bad because he doesn't struggle at all now, even in the toughest of subjects. He might actually be fine in college, too.

However, will that sense of security hold up when he's a chemical engineer and he has to respond immediately to a volatile situation in his lab? I don't know. Will my son know how to think for himself and problem solve without relying on something he was tested on to tell him how best to react? Again, I'm not sure.

I recently read an article about the idea of testing, and whether or not tests accurately measure intelligence or ability because my second son

T. Stasiuk / Flickr

is just the opposite. He fails on his tests. He feels stupid and has a low self-esteem. I have explained to him that his F's on his tests do not mean he doesn't understand or that he's not smart. It means he doesn't test well. There is a very interesting NY Times article focused on a study of children and what the authors think truly determines success that's titled What if the secret to success is failure? The URL for this site is at the end of the chapter.

Many people think that tests are worthless tools to measure what students know. Does that test measure how these students apply these multiple-choice answers to real problems they will need to solve in the future? I'd say no, it doesn't. There are so many articles published about students not getting essential critical thinking and problem-solving skills in school, let alone the ability to be creative. I think this is due to the lack of practical knowledge being instilled in students and a lack of presenting them with adequate opportunities to solve realistic problems while they are still learning. It is not the fault of teachers, because they all know better; it's the fault of our educational system and its dependence upon and nauseating defense of archaic methods of teaching, not to mention its means of evaluating what has been learned. I am half way up my soapbox, so I will hesitantly step down because that's best saved for another book.

Testing integrity online:

Traditional testing will never go away, and I will not assume that everyone ought to remove their traditional exams from their online courses and replace them with other forms of assessment. If you will still depend on traditional exams, you might want some help with test integrity. Many traditional teachers dislike online learning for one reason only, and that is that they fear one or more of the following: the student completing the work is not the student who registered, the student will cheat on the exams, and/or the student will share the exam questions with others. These things do happen and it might be no surprise to you that they happen in traditional classes too! Do you think a professor with a large lecture class of over 100 students knows who every student is? Unlikely. Do those professors check ID for every exam? I doubt it. There's no way to ensure the right person is being tested and no way to truly ensure the student is not cheating at all—whether it's old school or new school.

Specific techniques can be used to decrease the chances of cheating and student dishonesty. Here are a few of them★.

- Have the students sign an honor code at the beginning of the class

- Make all exams low-stakes—if the exam is 50% of the grade, or even 25%, the student might feel pressure to cheat

- Create a pool of questions from which each student's exam will pull when it comes time to their exam. This way not one student has the same questions

- The LMS might also allow you to 'randomize' questions, show one question at a time, prevent backtracking, limit the time on the test, require a password, and prevent students from seeing the correct answers until a specified date

- Keep the exam open for a specific time period, such as 3 full days. I wouldn't suggest an entire week, but also would not suggest only a few hours on one specified day

- Add to your exam questions on a regular basis so the exam is not the same each semester

- If your institution has an exam proctoring solution, use it

There are various high-tech and low-tech technology solutions that can help. You can require that one or more exams be 'proctored'. That's tough, though, if it's not an institutional mandate or supported initiative. The low-tech version is that students must come to campus or another 'approved' testing center to take the exam under the watchful eyes of someone else. That someone else has the password to the exam and checks the student's ID.

A high tech solution is using a Proctoring vendor. There are so many that I will not list them all here. Do a search and you will find several. Usually they are either a technology a student purchases that records him and the environment while the exam is on, a person who watches the student remotely while taking the exam, or a software that monitors the student for specific behaviors that might indicate dishonesty.

Authentic assessment:

Some people who frown upon traditional testing look toward authentic assessment as the alternative. Educause published a fantastic article on traditional versus authentic assessment (found at the conclusion of this chapter). You can find a convenient table that compares the two, but copyright issues prevent me from embedding it in this book. Essentially they support what it is that I am telling you here-- that students are going to be working in a different world than we were being prepared for-- one that is technology-focused, collaborative, innovative, and filled with new problems. Faculty members are responsible for preparing these students for that world, not the type that they were prepared for decades before.

I can understand the difficulty in rethinking assessment. After all, it's so much harder to think about alternatives to the traditional true/false and multiple-choice tests. Furthermore, many instructors use a Learning Management System to grade the tests, which is so nice for the instructor because it takes absolutely no time to grade them. I understand how appealing that is.

authentic

Definition: real, genuine

Synonyms: accurate, actual, authoritative, bona fide, certain, convincing, credible, creditable, dependable, factual, faithful, for real, legitimate, official, original, pure, reliable, sure, true, trust-worthy, trusty, twenty-four carat, valid, veritable

Notes: genuine means not fake or counterfeit - or sincerely felt or expressed, while authentic means conforming to fact and therefore worthy of belief and trust

Antonyms: counterfeit, fake, false, falsified, unauthorized, ungenuine, unreal

D. Bamford / Flickr

Not only that, but authentic assessment, besides being very time consuming to score, is so subjective. It's difficult to look at 25 different final projects to confidently determine that these students truly 'got it', that they can prove that they understand the subject matter, but also think independently, creatively, and critically. This isn't easy stuff.

So, what's authentic assessment? It's a lot of things. Again, Google it and you will find a lot of information and help. Essentially you create a project or task that the students will create or work on to prove what they know. It could be almost anything. If you re-visit chapter 5 you will see evidence of authentic assessment practices with the course projects I've had my students do. Granted, I am well aware that it's so much easier in my fields of expertise (English, Education), but nonetheless, there are resources out there to help you learn about authentic assessment. I will include some at the conclusion of this chapter. Think about this-- instead of asking your students to choose an answer to prove understanding, ponder a way to have them demonstrate it by doing something, creating something, or solving an actual problem in their fields.

This doesn't have to be an all-or-nothing deal. Go ahead and play around with the idea first to get comfortable with it. If you typically rely on traditional exams, remove one of them from your curriculum and replace it with a more authentic assessment★. Take it slow and see how it works for you. Look for various examples on the web in your subject area-- don't reinvent that wheel if something has already been created that gets you there.

Chapter Resources:

Educause article:
http://www.educause.edu/library/resources/making-grade-role-assessment-authentic-learning

Grant Wiggins: http://www.edutopia.org/grant-wiggins-assessment

Jon Mueller's Authentic Assessment Toolbox:
http://jfmueller.faculty.noctrl.edu/toolbox/whatisit.htm

New York Times Article:
http://www.nytimes.com/2011/09/18/magazine/what-if-the-secret-to-success-is-failure.html?pagewanted=all&_r=1&

University of Wisconsin-Stout Authentic Assessment site:

http://www.uwstout.edu/soe/profdev/assess.cfm

Chapter 7 checklist: Assessment

- o Don't create assessments until you have course outcomes and unit/weekly objectives
- o If you're going to use a traditional exam, make sure the questions are related to the objectives and outcomes
- o Discourage testing dishonesty through honor code signing, making exams low-stakes, pull from question pools, randomize questions, change exam questions often, or use a proctoring solution
- o Authentic assessments ask the students to *do* rather than to regurgitate facts
- o Start slow with authentic assessments if you have to; remove one quiz or exam and modify it to be more authentic

8

Give it some bling and make it sing!

If you are totally new to designing online courses and teaching online, read the second paragraph and then skip this chapter. Really. If you don't I will not be liable for the smoke that will inevitably start rising out of the top of your head. The rest of this chapter is for those who are comfortable with technology and course design to the point that they're ready to do something new and innovative with their content. However, if you're a newbie and still want to read about giving the course some bells and whistles, then feel free and read on.

Pictures are worth 1000 words:

I. Downing / Flickr

Before you delve into multimedia tools, make sure you include some images in your course content. You know, I didn't do that with this book until one of my reviewers (I will not mention names, but he's from Florida) suggested it. In a course and in books, images help break up the content and give the students/readers something interesting to look at while reading.

Some LMSs, like Canvas, have built-in image tools that make it quick and simple to search and add images (even with built-in ALT text for ADA compliance). For others, you have to get instructions from your cupcake-loving LMS administrator. Usually you can drag and drop, though. The important thing is for you to find creative commons licensed images. I used Flickr and Morgefile and made sure I chose ones that allowed commercial use for this book. Do not use Google images!

Pictures really do help students get engaged and interested in what you're sharing.

How to find tools and new things:

Besides images, there are so many tools available online to make your content more interesting and engaging that they can make even a seasoned techie motion sick with how quickly it all moves and changes. All you have to do is spend an hour or so on Twitter following folks like @edutopia , @edudemic, or search #edtech★. There are also many innovative teachers who are tearing up the twitter-verse with their influence in educational technology. You will find them if you're searching on educational technology. What these folks share are tools, news, research, and the "next best things" coming to education. Sometimes it's focused on K-12, sometimes higher ed, or a mix of both. This is how I tend to find the newest tools. Be sure that you're not breaking any rules, though, about using outside tools in your course. If your institution has policies about it, be sure to follow them.

There are some challenges to finding technology tools that can help you. Here's a list of them, although this is not at all exhaustive.

1. **Your operating system.** Some tools play well with only PCs. Typically you do not find tools that only work with Mac. You will find apps, though, that only work with Apple products.

2. **Your learning management system**. Some systems are built off of 'old' HTML code (Sakai, Moodle, and at this time, Blackboard) while some are 'new' HTML code (Canvas). Certain tools will work better with old code while others prefer new. Sometimes it's hard to know in advance whether something works well or not until you try.

3. **Your institution.** Do they support the use of extraneous tools that you find on the web? Sometimes they don't like it and prefer you use just what is available to you. Make sure you know what you're allowed to do, or just go rogue and take your chances.

4. **Money.** Yeah, they're not all free, although many good tools are (for now). Some of the really good products (like Articulate

Storyline) are expensive and that cost can be too prohibitive. Some aren't as pricey as Storyline, like Voicethread, which I love, but it still requires digging into the pocket, and an individual instructor might not be willing to do that. Other good things cost a small amount (like Screencast-o-matic, which is $15.00 a year), but are well worth the personal investment. Keep in mind that some tools you find will have a 'free' version, but a 'pro' version will cost you some money. I've found most pro versions worth the money.

5. **You.** Some tools have a bigger learning curve than others. Usually the more expensive the tool is, the more complicated it is to learn because you're paying for all the cool stuff it can do (which also takes time to learn). So, if you get easily frustrated and don't like trying to figure things out, you might find some challenges with some tools. Your skills will help you—what you can and can't do will help you decide what to choose as well.

Inventory then explore:

S. TerBurg / Flickr

Now that I got all of the doom-and-gloom out of the way, let's jump right into what to use to help you design a course worthy of praise and glory. First, you want to do a good review of what you already have. Do you have any multimedia at all? Take note of where you're using in terms of multimedia, and for my own purposes I consider multimedia as videos (interactive or not), infographics (interactive or not), virtual games, virtual learning tools (like flashcards), simulations, lessons with audio and video, and anything else interactive that students can "play" with, watch, or listen to in order to learn.

Once you take inventory of what you already have, look for your institution's technology department. See what you might have licenses for already★. I know at Indiana University we have a site called "IU Ware", which gives us access to so many technology tools and software—all free if we work at IU. Your institution might have site licenses for things, so

63

look there to see what treasures might be hidden. Once you find out, explore what's available to you (or not) and perhaps seek the assistance of someone in that department who can tell you more about what the software is, and its capabilities. You can also do a Google search to find out for yourself. Someone might even be available to teach you how to use the software.

Quantity and quality:

You might not be sure how much multimedia you need to include. There's no 'magic number' out there- no research that tells you how much is too little or too much, at least not yet. **When I train faculty to design online courses I suggest one piece of multimedia each week★**. This is a good place to begin. If you don't have any multimedia at all, start with every other week and build from there. The people with the least amount of experience with technology tend to choose videos as their multimedia- from YouTube, YouTube Edu, or TED.com★. These can be easily embedded in learning management systems to watch right from the screen and work with mobile devices. YouTube even has built-in closed captioning for ADA compliance.

I find it appealing when instructors offer a variety of multimedia. For example, one week it might be an audio file associated with a written lecture. The next week it's a video with an interactive component created using TedEd or Zaption, and the week after that it's an interactive voice discussion created with Voicethread. Variety keeps things interesting, right? However, if you're new and embedding a YouTube video felt like an award-winning accomplishment, go ahead and stick with that until you're ready to try something new.

Some of the coolest online learning courses I've seen include interactive lessons created with software programs like Lectora, Snap!, Articulate Storyline, and Adobe Captivate. This is a short list of a few that can do these things. Unfortunately, three out of the four of these take some time to learn. Snap (at this time) is a PC only program, which is unfortunate, and it's the easiest of the group to grasp. There are easier programs like Softchalk, but the output is not as flashy as those created by the others. If you have it, though, by all means, use it.

What I mean by 'interactive lesson' is a learning instance that includes text for students to read, audio they listen to, videos they watch, and

64

questions they answer (or text they move around). Objects can be clicked on and manipulated in an interactive lesson. The students can learn and then the lesson offers them a way to check their understanding through a quiz (that's graded or not) or other interactive ways to shove that knowledge deeper into their long-term memory. Creating these is quite advanced, so it might take time. The quickest way to try this out would be by exploring Ed.Ted.com, which is an easy (and free) way to create an interactive lesson, but at this time you can't embed them.

What else can you do with multimedia? Well, replace some of your PowerPoint presentations with Prezi's or PowToons★. PowToon also recently launched a new tool called Slides, which is a PowerPoint alternative! You can also use Screencast-o-matic to record yourself and your presentation. Make short lectures using this tool, upload into YouTube, and embed them in your course. Your online students will see you, hear you, and watch your presentation.

Let's see… you can also give your students projects like creating interactive timelines in history or literature★. Give them tools to use like MyHistro.com, or TimeGlider or you use them to share historical or other information related to events. Create learning games with

D. Brekke / Flickr

AdventureMaker, Jumpcraft, or custom crossword puzzles with JustCrosswords.com There is so much that you can do to break the cycle of reading, writing, and discussing. Get out there and play!

ADA compliance:

When it comes to multimedia, keep ADA in mind. Avoid using animated .gif files if at all possible. They are neat, but distracting to the visually challenged. If you make an audio file or record a video, write your script first. You don't have to read from it while recording, but provide a copy of the file with the audio/video for those who have issues hearing★. If you create snazzy little videos using tools that are just music with words on the screen (like with Animoto or PowToon), that's ok as long as the words appear long enough for a reasonable person to read them.

Browsers are wonky:

In addition to ADA, be aware that Internet browsers are wonky and something you create might look fine in Firefox, but disappear if you open it using Chrome. It's important that you always have two browsers available and make sure you inform your students of 1) which browser is best for your LMS and 2) the need to have two browsers★. Typically Firefox is the best for most LMSs and tools. Even so, a lot of objects you create are made using Javascript, so it's imperative that your Java is up-to-date. If you have automatic updates set up on your machine you should be ok, but it's good to check by visiting the Java website to check your version.

When you create these cool things, it's best to embed them versus just put a link in your course so your students have to go outside of the LMS to interact, watch, or listen★. Embedding varies widely with the LMS you have, but almost always it means getting an embed code from the object, and being able to get into HTML mode to embed it. I won't get into how to do that, but will tell you to bring another cupcake to LMS person and ask him or her to show you how to embed something. You can offer that person good advice, too, by suggesting that if there aren't any short 'how to' videos on things such as this that the LMS person makes them for the faculty.

Where do you get these?

By now you're probably wondering when I'm going to tell you what all of these tools are, right? I won't give that to you because in less than a year the list will be outdated. Instead, I will suggest two things. First, email me (justcallmeang@hotmail.com) and ask me for my own Bells & Whistles list★. If you bought this book I will send it to you for free; if I gave this book away, then I will charge you $5.00.

Hopefully you didn't believe me because I'm just kidding! ☺ I thought about including it **in** this book, but, again, it would be outdated too quickly. I will send it to you if you ask. This way you have the most up-to-date version. I created this list in 2009 and have been adding to it, removing tools, and making adjustments as needed. Most of the tools I have on the list are free.

The second thing you can do is visit this website: http://c4lpt.co.uk/top100tools/★. Jane Hart keeps this list going and each year more and more people vote on their top tools. The final thing you can do is Google some of the tools I suggested in this chapter. You will find them, I promise. The apps that only work with apple products are not included on either list, for the most part. I love Tellagami, an iPad or Android app that helps you create cute audio announcements with an animated avatar and a background★. It's free.

Another is Explain Everything, which helps you show students how to do something- anything, really, with audio and a recording of what you do on the iPad screen★. What would be best is to do a search for the "best apps for higher ed" or "best apps for K12 teachers". Specify your search. Find the app that fits your device—android or iOS. They will come and go, cost you something or not, and will change as quickly as the weather in Northwest Indiana.

My final thoughts for this chapter are that it's ok to keep your course simple, but don't let yourself stagnate there. Each time you teach I'd like for you to try something new to make your course better. Use a new tool every 6 months or so. Once you learn it, use it or you will forget it. It takes time, I know, but it will keep your brain young.

I also encourage you to attend conferences that focus on technology. You will learn so much from them that you'll come home swimming with ideas. The best one I have attended is the Emerging Technologies for Online Learning conference (ET4Online) that's offered by OLC (formally Sloan-C) and Merlot★. When you learn something new and feel confident in your skills, teach others. Offer to give a brown bag workshop at your institutions. Spread your excitement. You'd be amazed at what could happen to the institutional culture when people share their enthusiasm and knowledge with each other.

Chapter 8 checklist: Bells, Whistles, and Bling

- Use images in your courses, but use ALT Text for ADA
- Find out what site licenses your institution has for multimedia software
- Consider including one piece of multimedia each week
- Replace Power Point presentations with cooler things like Prezi, PowToon, Slides, or screencasts
- If you make an audio recording or video, record a written script first for ADA
- If you use neat learning tools, embed them whenever possible
- Email Angela to get her bells & whistles document (justcallmeang@hotmail.com)
- Keep track of this website: http://c4lpt.co.uk/top100tools/
- Try a new technology tool each time you teach your course
- Attend conferences that focus on technology, like ET4Online

9

It's showtime!

Waifer X / Flickr

I can remember well the first time I taught online. It was for Westwood College Online and it was an introductory writing course. I was fortunate to have had the course already designed for me and I had to go through mandatory training that prepared me for the school's expectations, which were that I remained engaged in the course discussions, answered student questions quickly, graded efficiently with a reasonable turnaround time, and provided the students with feedback on all the work that I graded.

It seemed simple enough, but I still remember being very nervous and unsure about what I had gotten myself into. However, I remember how quickly I found a routine, how much I enjoyed the online interactions with my students, and how surprised I was at the learning community that developed. I never turned back, like I said in the first chapter.

For you, perhaps you've already taught online and you're over your stage fright. That's wonderful. For those who aren't over it, do know that it's very normal to feel uncertain and that feeling is likely very new and foreign, especially if you've been teaching for quite some time traditionally. Your confidence will grow with experience, but I can't promise you that your confidence will increase by leaps and bounds the first time around, especially if you were the person designing your own course.

More than once I mentioned the importance of making sure your course is fully designed before you teach it. Another reason why is that you will need to spend your time doing things other than worrying about getting more weeks of content online before the students are looking for them. Thinking about teaching online and what that means for you on a daily basis is usually more stressful than the reality of the situation. The reality is that most of your time will be (or should be) spent participating in your course, grading and providing feedback, and answering questions★.

Answering questions:

Students will inevitably have questions. The best thing to do is have a discussion forum that is just for questions. Call it what you want, such as Virtual Office, Q&A Forum, Ask the Prof, whatever you want. Always keep it at the top. Inform the students that all course questions that are not personal should be asked there. Tell them that you do not accept non-personal email questions! You will get too many emails. Plus, having a forum dedicated to questions will help you revise the course later. Areas of confusion will show you what needs clarification.

V. Everett / Flickr

I can't stress how important it is that you check this forum as often as you can, and 15 minutes is sufficient to check for questions. If your LMS allows you to 'subscribe' to that forum and get emails when posts are made, please subscribe. This way you get the email and can go in and answer the question within a reasonable time frame. If you want, allow students to answer questions posted there if they know the answer. That's up to you.

A few ways to decrease the amount of student questions you get are★:

- Have a student orientation video in the first week that shows them how to navigate the course, where to turn in assignments, how to get their grades, etc.

- Have a syllabus quiz in the first week that forces them to read the syllabus and the expectations

- Design an easy-to-navigate course that has been reviewed by at least one other person

Participating:

In order to avoid burnout, remember that you do not need to be online constantly. Students might expect that, surely, but that is not suggested. Instead, schedule your time online just like you would any other activity that you do regularly. Try to log in every single day during the week just to check for questions★. This does not mean that you log in for several hours each day; like I said a few paragraphs ago, 15 minutes is sufficient just to check. If you want to take a day completely 'off", like Saturday or Sunday, be sure to include that information in your syllabus so students know. In addition to checking for questions, other time should be spent participating. To do this efficiently, consider the following:

- If you require your students to participate 2 or 3 days a week, so should you.

- Set aside time to check discussions and reply, either to individual students if your class is small, or to groups or students in general if you have a large class.

- If you do have a decent class size and you want to respond to each student each week, create a checklist from your roster. Print enough copies for each week and mark off to whom you've responded. It gets difficult to try and remember, even in a class of 10 (trust me).

- Participating should take about 30 minutes each time you log in. Make sure you mark all posts you read as "read" to avoid confusion about what you've read or not the next time.

- You do not need to read every post students make. You do not need to respond to every post a student makes. Really.

- Use student names every chance you can get when posting to the class or to individuals.

71

- Save all general comments you make each week, as you might be able to re-use them when you teach it again and that will save time in the future.

Grading:

R. Hyde / Flickr

Besides answering questions and participating, you will spend a lot of time grading. This might not be true for the folks who primarily use LMS-graded quizzes or tests as their assessments of choice. For them, grading isn't much of a hassle. Since you probably read Chapter 5, and from that you probably should have remembered that having those assessments probably isn't the best way to assess what your students have learned, you are probably of the notion that grading will indeed take you some time (or I'm secretly wishing that it's so).

In previous chapters I shared with you that you do need to pay close attention to what you are assigning because you have to grade what you assign. Each week that you do not have a major exam or project due you should have some form of discussion or interaction that is graded★. Go back to Chapter 6 to get tips and tricks on grading discussion effectively and efficiently. I also shared with you that it is imperative that you provide your students with grading criteria for all course assignments. You will use those criteria while grading, so ease of use is crucial to save you time.

If you have 3 items to manually grade each week, the task could seem daunting. I know; I've been there many times. You do want to provide your students with an accurate assessment of their work, and provide them with feedback, but sometimes you will struggle because time might be running out. There are people who teach online who are somehow able to grade the day following the week ending. Wow… they impress me. For myself, though, I need a little breather before I jump right into that. Do spread your grading out a bit over the week so it's not overwhelming. That's the first thing for you to do.

Make certain that no more than 7 days pass between when an assignment is due and when you grade it. Students will expect you to grade immediately★. I'm totally serious. They will turn it in on Tuesday (it's due Sunday) and by Thursday will ask you why you haven't graded their assignment. This happens with faculty too! Even though I tell them that all assignments will be graded after the week has ended, somehow they either don't read it, don't notice it, or forget.

Usually I will grade discussion first. That grade usually gets feedback. If I have smaller assignments like my reading reflections that are pretty much complete/not complete, I don't usually give feedback with the grade unless they get less than the full points. If I only have two assignments to grade, then I will provide them with a short comment on what they wrote. The larger assignments typically get graded over 2 to 3 days. I have average-sized classes, so I break them up for my own sanity. My goal is to have everything graded by Friday night when the week ends on a Sunday.

Paper grading takes the longest amount of time for most people, whether you're teaching online or getting them the old-school way. In the online environment, though, there are some things that can make it less ominous and time-consuming. First, see what your LMS can do to save you time. Canvas was the first LMS to have "Speedgrader", which

J. Guldi / Flickr

is really cool. The papers/assignments appear without you having to click on them to download them. You can do simple marks on the page (typed comments, strike outs, etc.) and you can record audio comments too. Now Blackboard has something similar in the more recent versions.

Do be sure to check on what document types work best in these LMSs since that changes sometimes. Canvas was also the first to have an integrated rubric feature so that if you have a rubric associated with an assignment, it appears in the Speedgrader window so you click boxes, it tallies the points, and you're set unless you're giving written comments too. I know other LMSs out there have some of these features, so explore what yours can do to save you time.

A simple technique is to make sure you don't assign ridiculously long papers. After all, how much is enough? Figure that out. Regardless of the length of the papers, use marks on them judiciously. I am not convinced students actually pay a whole lot of attention to tiny marks like comma splices or sentence fragments or an incorrect use of a possessive. I think they'd prefer to read what you thought about their content rather than all of those marks that look like chicken pox on paper. So, think about avoiding your tendency to mark them and focus on writing feedback or filling in the rubric for the paper. I say this and laugh because I have this horrible tendency to do exactly what it is I'm telling you not to do. I will work on it if you do.

If you can't help yourself, though, think about getting Annotate for Word College Edition Pro. You get it through a company called 11trees.com★. I think it works best on PC (as of right now) although there is a Mac version that isn't as easy to use. The cost is minimal and it is downloaded on your computer as an add-on to Microsoft Word. It adds a new ribbon and hundreds of built-in comments and help on everything you can think of. Literally, you find an area of concern (like an incorrectly formatted MLA citation), you put your cursor there, then go to the ribbon, find the section on research, then MLA, then click the box that relates to in text citations. It populates a comment that says the citation is incorrect and gives them a website to visit that helps them fix it (usually the Purdue OWL).

Those who like techie things can also think about providing audio feedback on the paper. Bring the paper up on the screen and make comments while you're reading and record your comments using any tool you can think of. If you want to record the screen with the paper on it and your voice, then use something like Screencast-o-matic. See Chapter 9 for technology tools like this one.

Course Maintenance:

While the course is running you might find yourself realizing a few things, like a specific assignment just isn't working right, or a discussion question needs to be modified, a rubric adjusted, or other things like this. You might drive yourself crazy if you try and fix everything once the

74

week has passed. Instead, consider keeping an electronic note going on your computer, your phone, or tablet★. Keep track of what you want to change so that once you get a break in the semester, you can go back in and fix things. Plus, by the time the course is over and the entire context of the class and its parts are very clear, your perspective might change a little, so be patient and 'fix' later.

If your course has low enrollment:

Small courses can be wonderful, but it takes work to make it so. If the small course is graduate-level, it will be easier for you since the students are expected to be self-motivated individuals who have been in college before and generally know what's expected. A small undergraduate course might be more challenging. The biggest issue you will face at either level is keeping the course 'moving'.

In average courses there are enough people 'talking' throughout the week that there's almost always something going on. If you have a class with only 10 students, or even less than 10, you may have a group that is mostly 'last minute posters' and if so, that will create some stagnation. Further, you will really depend on the small group of students to do what they're supposed to do when they're supposed to do it. Regular, engaging, interactive discussions are vital for the students to get the most out of the course.

You will need to inform the class in advance that the small class size means they're all responsible for making it work well. Empower them to make the course amazing. Be sure you require discussion postings by mid-week so that the discussion isn't just happening over the weekends. Encourage them to get more involved—have them pose additional questions, find resources, etc. This will help pad the interaction a bit.

Your role will increase a bit in the small course because you will need to make sure they know you're there too, as the feeling of isolation will be greater in a small online course. Spend extra time giving them feedback; send them nice encouraging emails if you notice them going above and beyond. Reaching out to them personally will benefit them and the course community.

I would avoid group projects in small courses. I don't think that you would want to risk a group project if you have less than 6 people per group, because if students withdraw or just disappear, the other students will experience increased anxiety and pressure to tow the line. Those are emotions that are not conducive to positive online course experiences.

When you have a large enrollment online course:

I hope that if you are stuck with a large online class that it's not your first online teaching experience. If so, that's too bad; you should refrain from judging "online learning" as a thing, as an experience, until you teach an average-sized course a few times. I know there are many reasons why institutions have large online classes, and it's my hope that they don't do if they don't absolutely have to, because the student and faculty experience suffers. If they can't help it (and, let's face it, in this economy with education lacking funding, this is a reality), then you have to do what you have to do. Listen, it's not the end of the world and you CAN do it.

The same quality design suggestions I've already presented still apply. Have your course ready to go in advance, make it interactive, engaging, interesting, and filled with opportunities to "DO" things and interact with each other. How they do these things and how they interact, including how you assess these things they do, will probably need to be adjusted for the large class.

- Be sure to have some information in that first week about being a successful online learner—like tips and tricks, things to remember, how to manage their time, and how to navigate the course and/or LMS

- Put students into discussion groups or learning teams before the class even begins. It's easiest for you and for grading purposes to do this by last name

- In your LMS discussion forum, put the discussion question(s) in there, and then start a discussion thread for each group or team. For the first week, put their last names in there. Here's an example:

  Group 1: Adams, Beecham, Cookman, Diehl, Effram, Franks
  Group 2: Goodrum, Hahn, Jackman, Kline, Ling, Marks

- For all other weeks, just put the group/team name as a discussion thread

- Make sure your expectations for discussions are very clear. Do not require too much or too little each week

- Explain to the students, in advance, how discussions will work so they're not overwhelmed or confused

- Give them some examples of HOW to participate in discussions. They may not understand what to do. Refer back to the chapter about discussions for some tips you can use for your own students

- Consider assigning group/team projects. One could be that the group is responsible for teaching the class a particular subject and they need to create a virtual learning supplement for the unit in which the subject is covered. It is vitally important, though, to give individual grades even for group work or your students will hate it. They will work harder too

- Use grading rubrics when you grade everything. More than likely you might have to forego individualized feedback on some assignments unless you have access to a TA or two

- Peer review works really well here too. Just make sure you give them criteria to use when evaluating their peers' work—a rubric would be even better

- Do not allow late work. This will be a nightmare if you do. If you want to show some flexibility, then drop the lowest score on something

- As much as I don't like suggesting it, you might need to change some of your authentic assignments to more traditional assessment methods like LMS-graded tests or quizzes, but I warn you to avoid making them high-stakes. Keep the points reasonable to discourage cheating (OR allow collaboration on tests/quizzes)

- You can and should participate regularly. Just pop into the groups and make general group comments rather than individual posts. Do still use student names, though, as often as you can

- Anticipate the questions students will have about the class and perhaps create a FAQ page. Consider including what happens when they submit an assignment to know if it went through, how long you will take to respond to a question, email, or assignment, and other things. Tell them early to review the FAQ before submitting a question

- Use announcements every week. The announcement should tell the students what will be going on that week and how it relates to what you've already done and/or what they will do in coming weeks

- I've already mentioned how important it is for you to have personalized learning material for your students—that is, like a lecture (but much shorter) from you. Take it one step further like Roger Berry did from California State University.

Roger realized that his undergraduate students struggled some with the text they had to read, so he created "study buddy notes" that went along with the textbook readings★. He would indicate a page and then give them a little tidbit like "On page 200, this material is complex and confusing, so read this comment from me before you read that part of the chapter…" He would infuse comments where needed, especially if he had information that wasn't in the textbook. See the references section of the book for an article that you can search and read on your own about managing large online classes.

Chapter 9 checklist: Course Management

- Most of your time will be spent participating, grading, providing feedback, and answering questions
- Have a discussion forum just for questions; allow students to answer them if they can; subscribe to it if you're able
- Participate as often as you tell them to participate
- Use student names when you grade and comment

- Save general comments in a folder
- Spread out grading so it's not overwhelming
- Students will expect you to grade immediately after they turn something in
- Consider grading discussion first
- Paper grading can be arduous, so if you have control over paper length, be smart about how long you ask them to be
- Annotate for Word Pro from 11trees.com is great for paper grading
- Keep notes of things that need major changes, like assignments, and fix them after the course is over

In small enrollment online courses:

- Require discussion posts by mid-week
- Empower the students to make the course awesome even with a small number of people
- Your role will increase a bit in small courses because you will need to stay on top of them to post and interact
- Group projects might not be the best idea

In large enrollment online courses:

- Make sure you provide adequate help in advance for being successful in the online class
- Group students for discussions and possibly projects (maybe 10 to a group)
- You might have to have more LMS graded assessments in large classes ☹
- When students are in group discussions, make group comments instead of individual comments
- Create a FAQ page/section that is easily found (maybe in a "start here" section)
- Use announcements weekly

10

The dog ate my homework and I hate democrats

M. Black / Flickr

If you've taught at all, at any level, you know that one of the biggest issues you have to deal with is students not doing the work that is assigned, doing it incorrectly, or turning it in late. It's just human nature to make excuses about situations that are potentially threatening (such as hearing, "too bad, it's a zero") to lessen the probability of hearing an undesirable or devastating consequence.

We get started with those behaviors at a very young age. I recall a story told to me by my paternal grandmother. I was less than 3 years old and decided to 'feed' my one year old little brother an entire chocolate chip cookie. I shoved it in his mouth so far that he couldn't chew it (he didn't really have many teeth at the time anyway), and thus started choking. She said my response was, "him said he was hungry". Well, there you have it. Excuses are everywhere and definitely something for which you will need preparation in an online class.

In face-to-face classes your students see you. They cannot hide behind a computer; they cannot 'fake' as much as they can when they never have to look you in the eye. There's a freedom from that dreadful feeling of having to face the person to whom you've lied (or are about to lie) in order to get out of an assignment or to get an extension. Because of that drastic difference in interpersonal interaction, students seem to be more likely to pull excuses out of hats, sometimes even outrageous ones. After all, will you check everything they claim? Will you ask for proof? Most people wouldn't, especially in an uncomfortable situation like the death of a family member. I can't even begin to tell you some of them. I am a member of an online Facebook group for people who teach online and some of the student excuses presented have made my face blush and my mouth drop like, "Is this even for real?" and, indeed, it always is.

There's a fine line you need to walk when you teach online. You want to be firm, have standards and expectations, but you also don't want to appear authoritarian and unapproachable. Well, at least I wouldn't think you'd want that. I used to be way too soft. I am generally a softhearted person and I have been burned many times by people who take advantage of this part of my nature. However, I have had to grow some longer teeth in my teaching years to protect my convictions and expectations. I'm not mean, but I'm much more direct, explicit, and firm from the start of the course.

Breaking the excuse machine:

In order to discourage the excuse machine from running amuck in your online course, have guidelines in your syllabus about late work, incomplete work, missed exams, or missed assignments★. I have covered this in a previous chapter, but it is worth repeating that you need to set a policy and stick to it. Have that policy covered on a syllabus quiz or a contract that the students sign, so you know and they know that the expectations are clear. I've also told you the joy of grace periods for grading—giving them "until you grade" (usually an extra 2-3 days for me) seriously decreased the amount of excuses I've had to deal with.

I think it helps to approach it in a matter-of-fact way—that you know things happen, that things have happened in your life too, but sometimes you have to accept it and just move on. Making excuses is not something anyone wants to make a habit. Be accountable and revisit priorities so it doesn't happen again. Again, you can be firm without coming off as a heavy-handed control freak without a heart.

Another way of discouraging these issues is by making sure your course isn't packed too full with work. If students have too much going on, and they're overwhelmed with work, something will have to give at some point. Revisit previous chapters that discuss work load and make sure you don't have too much assigned each week. In addition, make sure you're giving them enough time to complete assignments. The amount of time they have should depend on what's involved. Heavy research (at least quality research) is time consuming, so ensure you're considering that in your course design.

Other student issues:

If you're lucky you will not encounter any 'problem' students during your course. I know I haven't had them very often, but I have had them. When you do, usually you don't forget them. I will provide a few examples of 'challenging' students you might encounter at some point and provide you with some advice about dealing with them. While I know it's not nice to label anyone with a specific title, and I do not label people as a personal habit, this is the easiest way for me to help you by categorizing a specific 'student'.

Of course, any student can do any of these things at any time, and a bad choice does not make a student a bad person. I want to qualify this before I get horrible emails. With that part complete, let's move on to the issues. Keep in mind that what I suggest below is not **the** right way in every situation; it's just a suggestion. Make sure you know your campus rules and guidelines for dealing with student issues first; then, you can always seek the assistance of other faculty, your administration, or even Google the problem to see what others have done.

The "I'm-stuck-in-my-beliefs-and-everyone-else-is-wrong" student

This is probably the most prevalent problem online because people who might not speak up in any other circumstance must speak up in an online class. Thus, everyone has an equal voice at all times. Plus, there's no fear of public judgment or persecution. Even if other students 'write' negative responses, they're not even close to the same as a face-to-face, in a crowd, type of confrontation. So, students who hold strong beliefs about anything—especially religion and politics—might feel compelled to express them, even if it means being impolite, judgmental, or offensive to others.

Some courses are ready-made for political, religious, and other controversial subjects. For those instructors in those disciplines, beware. There's something wonderful about healthy discourse that is controversial, absolutely, and an online class is perfect to get students to deeply explore and evaluate issues from various perspectives. Don't avoid the conversation; prepare the students in advance for 'acceptable' communication, 'unacceptable' communication, and the consequences thereof.

This is a great time to discuss critical thinking and exploring one's own deeply held beliefs that generally go unquestioned and unevaluated because "this is the way I was raised" or "this is the *right* way to think". If you have the opportunity, create a lesson about evaluating one's assumptions. Have the students think about and explore from where these strong beliefs originated, whether or not these beliefs should be questioned, whether they're based upon facts and direct experiences, or based upon family, religious, or cultural biases and prejudices. Sure, you're not going to change what they think (or probably not), but just opening that door to self-reflection, self-critique, is a good start.

In order to keep the class environment healthy, give them specifics about what's ok to say and what's not. It's ok to say what you think as long as it is not directed at a person, a culture, a group of people that would find it offensive or hurtful. For example, if you're covering gay rights, and you have a few students who have strong religious convictions, prepare yourself for what might be said. If you nip the issue in the bud, though, it

should be ok. Those students can say, "My religion has taught me that a relationship with someone of the same sex is wrong because …" Then, it's ok for another student to ask that student to personally justify that belief. Who says it's wrong? How do you know for sure?

E. Simpson / Flickr

I know someone very well that hates Democrats. He puts all Democrats in the same hole—they're "bleeding heart liberals" who want to keep people dependent. In a healthy discourse, it's great to question strong beliefs by asking questions like, "Do you feel comfortable labeling every Democrat in the world as a 'bleeding heart liberal'?" "Why?" "Is it the person you hate, or is it what you assume they all believe?" I hope you see what I'm getting at here. People will have strong opinions, but you need to teach them how to voice them in an appropriate way and also teach them it's good to question each other and themselves.

If a student still posts something offensive to the class, be sure to make a copy of it before you do anything else★. Take a screen shot, that's the best thing. Then, remove the post. Contact the student and explain what crossed the line and perhaps how the student could have said it in a more appropriate way. Or, ask the student to suggest a revised way of expressing her opinion. If a specific student was targeted, contact him and explain that you noticed an inappropriate comment and that you took care of the situation. The entire class will need a reminder about acceptable and unacceptable language/content.

The overachiever

I think I've had more of these students (and the slackers) than anything. Being an overachiever is a behavior with which I can personally associate. I can't help it either. However, if a student takes his or her drive to an unhealthy level, or if the student overtakes the course in some respects, it might force you to intervene.

Most of my overachieving students fit into one or more of these categories: 1) a non-traditional age student, generally over the age of 25, but usually over the age of 30; 2) military; 3) a returning student who has failed to complete college at a previous attempt; 4) a 'teacher' pleaser. I have had younger students, though, who work extremely hard and try their best to impress me. I love seeing these students and enjoy my interactions with them and I am sure you will too.

These students will always turn in their work on time, will be the first to post in discussion, will post much more than is expected of them and exceed expectations, will want to know specifically what you're looking for and seek to exceed your highest expectations. They are usually very supportive of other students and offer substantive feedback to the students they choose to review when it comes time to peer review. They help make the class run smoothly.

So, how does it go badly? You might need to intervene when the student posts too much in discussion. This is a difficult situation because you really shouldn't discourage students, so you will have to be careful about approaching this. The way I would approach it might look something like this,

"Mark, you have such wonderful things to say in discussion, and your posts are some of the best I've ever read. Can you do me a favor, though, and hold back just a little because the other students are slightly intimidated and I can see that they aren't posting much because they feel like they can't possibly measure up to you? Thank you for your dedication to being the best student you can!"

You might also have to deal with the student and his approach to assignments. This student might see a requirement of 5 pages and give you 8. Encourage your overachiever to follow the guidelines. Make it a personal challenge to him. Don't threaten reduced points or anything like that, but suggest that it would be a personal goal for that student to revise and reduce.

Finally, the overachiever will definitely provide the best peer reviews when that is assigned in class. Sometimes, though, that presents a challenge for the student because in my experience the overachievers have a hard time understanding why other students don't 'get it' like they do, or why some students can't seem to write a paragraph without sentence fragments and misspelled words. You will need to encourage all students to provide constructive feedback and be careful with their tone. Deal with this if you have to on a one-on-one basis. It's a good idea to keep any eye on peer reviews in case it gets offensive instead of constructive.

The habitual slacker

Oh, goodness, where do I begin? This type of student is different from the "woefully underprepared". This student is prepared and knows what online learning is, but just doesn't seem to get a handle on time management. Usually this manifests itself early in the semester. These students tend to be late to log in to the course the first week and continue to lag behind or disappear at different times during the course. In all honesty you will know who these students are pretty quickly in your course.

I have not been able to find a specific strategy to decrease the amount of slackers or increase the likelihood that the slacking student will turn things around and do well. It's very situational and personal with the specific student that is having issues. One thing that would make a big difference is reaching out to the student during the first week. If it's close to the end of the first week (if the week begins on Monday, like Thursday or Friday) and a student or two (hopefully no more than 3) haven't logged in, please contact those students★. Email is fine. If you prefer the phone, then do that too, but definitely send an email with something like, "Have you forgotten about us?" Keep it upbeat, ask the student what's keeping her from logging in, and ask how you can help.

There comes a time, though, that the warm fuzzies are thrown out the window and you do need to deal with business. Students need to understand what's expected and what will happen if they can't meet those expectations.

T. Green / Flickr

Your institution ought to have a policy about 'attendance' online; if not, they need to in order to comply with some federal regulations on financial aid. Some schools allow faculty members to automatically withdraw students who just aren't cutting it. Make sure students know this. Auto dropping helps save financial aid funds and keeps students from signing up for classes that do not want to actually complete it. If your school doesn't have this option, then do whatever you can under the policies that govern this area.

Some students who slack do so because they just don't have the skills they need to manage life and school. I feel very strongly that institutions need to prepare every student for online learning and academic expectations. I love it when I see a mandatory online course for all students that focuses on strategies for managing life, school, time, and dealing with typical academic skills needed in all courses. I know there's research out there proving that a course like this affects attrition rates. Maybe the students just need to learn how to prioritize their life and stay focused on their goals.

Usually what happens with me is I will have students who just barely hang on. They will be late with some things, not turn in some work, but they don't quite fail. No matter what I've done, the student just does the minimum. I can't take these situations personally and neither can you. Sometimes there's nothing you can do. I won't hand hold anyone, but I am lenient the first week and make sure I am kind and communicative. What's important is that you stick to your expectations and consequences even though it's inevitable that the slacking student will have many excuses as to why the work is late, can't be done, or is completed incorrectly.

Hail the entitled one

People who act entitled annoy me. It's just one of my pet peeves and unfortunately I see it so often in young people today that it might become the new 'normal'. I certainly hope not, though. I have not experienced entitlement with my non-traditional students, but I won't say that it can't happen. It just depends on the student. Generally speaking I see more entitlement behaviors with traditional age college students, those who are

B. Dunnette / Flickr

less than 23 or so years old. Regardless of the age, sex, race, or circumstances of the student, entitlement behaviors elicit a strong reaction from me.

If you experience this (and perhaps you have in face to face classes), usually it's a student who thinks he deserves a certain grade and you did not give him that grade. It could also manifest itself

if the student made some kind of mistake (such as forgot a due date, misunderstood an assignment, posted less than was expected, that sort of thing). The student might expect that you do what he wants, such as allowing an extension, allowing a re-do, etc. In addition, if you don't do what the student wants, he might have a tantrum. Some of these students express themselves within the online course to other students in discussion forums (yes, even though you can read these comments); sometimes they contact department heads and complain. Be prepared because when the entitlement runs deep, there's not much the student wouldn't do to get his way.

I don't have much in terms of wisdom here because there's not a lot you can do except stick to your guns and realize that if the student's parents didn't discipline adequately and helped manifest these behaviors, then there's little you can do to change that student. Reality will do that at some point. For you, though, be kind yet firm. I strongly suggest you do not give in unless you *should* (due to your own error)★. If the student is being publically inappropriate, you will need to deal with it swiftly. Make copies of everything that was posted (screenshots are best), remove the postings, contact the student, and potentially involve student affairs. Do not allow a disgruntled student to single-handedly disrupt your learning community.

The woefully underprepared:

It is very sad that we still get college students who cannot write complete sentences, or students who think that to research means to type something into Google and put it in their paper. It's horrible that students are unable to think for themselves, critically analyze media messages, and provide a thoughtful reflection without being interrupted with text messages, Facebook notifications, Snapchat sounds, and Instragram posts. Students are very, very different and the ones in K-12 right now will come to college and probably resemble aliens to us once they get there. Not only do we have to deal with students not having academic skills that they need, but we are also dealing with attention spans that decrease every single year, the need for instant gratification, demand for constant entertainment, and socially-accepted electronic addictions. Our technological successes can lead to academic failures.

It might seem like I'm blaming ill-prepared students on technology. That's not true, but I do think that students have so much constant access to it that they would rather be on the phone or the Xbox than read a book, spend time researching material for a paper, or do any school work that bores them. I do think our schools have work to do in terms of adequately preparing high school students for college work, but if the schools teach it, and the student doesn't learn it, then it might not be the school's fault.

I feel especially qualified to speak to preparation because I taught introductory composition for such a long time, both online and face to face, for schools in Indiana, Illinois, and online schools that had students from everywhere! I have had so many students in my career and the ones who are not prepared struggle so much just to figure out how to write grammatically correct sentences let alone how to perform in-text citations and write a Works Cited page properly.

The underprepared student is another student that you can't change. You can't give that student what she needs to be better equipped for your class. What you can do, though, is help her find resources to improve her skills. Point her to the writing center. If you don't have any tutoring available online, perhaps you can rally to get something. Students do need it and will use it. Smarthinking is one with which I am most familiar and I have been very thankful for its services for my students in the past. Make sure you provide the students with on-campus tutoring help if the students are near a campus★. Give the student links to sites that help with specific skills like grammar, punctuation, research, citing, time management, and help with the Learning Management System.

Finally, see what you can do about encouraging your institution to provide a mandatory online class for all students. It can be short, but effective. It should introduce key academic skills that will help those students throughout their college journeys and life skills that can result in transformation of someone's life and future★.

The plagiarizer

Hopefully if you do have a student that plagiarizes, she won't do it

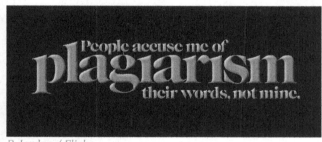

B. Jordan / Flickr

more than once. I have had a student repeat this mistake once that I can remember, but that's unusual. I think plagiarism is so rampant that it's something that happens right under your nose more often than you think. Ideally your institution will have a plagiarism detection service built in to your LMS so that you can automatically check all written assignments without blinking an eye. If not, though, you're on your own to check them. Google has been the best thing for me. I read the assignment, and if I suspect something funky going on, I will copy an entire sentence and paste it into Google to see what happens★. About 90 % of the time my instincts are spot on.

I will definitely stop grading if an entire paragraph is copied and will give the student a 0 and share the site or sites that were plagiarized. If it's just a sentence or two I do not give a 0, but give the student a scolding about copying and pasting, reduce the points, and hope the student learns his lesson. If it's the first time and the first paper I might give the student a chance to redo the paper. This is usually met with relief, but that's your discretion. Please be aware that your institution might have its own policies about this and you need to follow those policies.

I don't think all students do this on purpose. Perhaps they weren't taught any better (or they were, but it didn't sink in). I'm not sure at what age or grade level plagiarism is generally taught. I remember watching my stepson "write" a paper about an arctic animal a few years back. He was in 6th grade and he literally copied and pasted information from websites. I questioned him and he said it was ok to his teacher. I said, "it's never ok because you didn't write this". I would bet he was given an A on that paper because even his teacher didn't think to check. When my own kids write things I force them to cite and show them how to properly reference material. I am certain their teachers know what I'm up to, but I'd rather my kids know now than pay the price later. So, the lesson here is to make sure your students know what it is during the first week, how to avoid it, and what will happen if they take the chance and plagiarize★.

I have found that online students try it a whole lot more often than face to face students, but if you have students turn papers in versus submit them electronically, I'd be confident you'd have some plagiarism going on too since it's much more difficult to check papers that are in your hand (although I still did it with Google by typing in questionable sentences). Make sure you put the fear of a powerful spiritual entity in them early on. That typically works for me, but not 100% of the time. Go back to the chapter about the syllabus and you can see my plagiarism policy.

These typical student problems are not exhaustive. There are others. Hopefully you've learned some strategies to help you deal with them when you're affected. Also, if you have other methods that work for you, please let me know and your name might appear in a future version of this book!

Chapter 10 checklist: Student excuses and issues

- Have policies and guidelines that are loophole free and STICK TO THEM
- Consider having grace periods for assignments to avoid excuses
- Have someone review your course to make sure you're not over-assigning work
- Online discussions give students freedom to express feelings and beliefs they otherwise would not in a face-to-face environment; be prepared for that
- Have built-in critical thinking and self-reflection activities to encourage students to reflect on their own assumptions, biases, and roots of beliefs
- Allow overachievers to overachieve
- Try your best to reach out to slacker students right away, but don't expect to change them
- Entitled students will challenge you; keep a clear syllabus, grading criteria or rubrics, and document everything
- Students might be under prepared for your class. Have some guidance that first week for dealing with the LMS, perhaps even how to set goals and manage time
- Plagiarism will happen
- Use Google if you don't have a plagiarism detection tool

11

Ice cream sandwich, anyone?

I'm a big fan of ice cream—and I do really love those ice cream sandwiches, especially when you let the ice cream melt just a little, removing that harsh firmness so the cookie is softer and the ice cream doesn't squish out everywhere when you bite in.

R. Daily / Flickr

Anyway, it also provides a great metaphor for quality feedback. This applies to any form of feedback—online courses, face-to-face courses, or even in the workforce. Students want to know what you think of their work, not just receive a letter or points. Even more, if the students do not get full credit, but are not given an explanation, they will wonder what they could have done better to get higher points next time. It is your job to ensure that your students always know what they did well, and what needs improving. The delicious middle part of your feedback is like the center of your ice cream sandwich; between two sweet cookie layers is what the students will get that they probably won't want to hear, but if you make sure it's a little soft around the edges it will cause less mess in the long run.

The time factor:

Again, just like participating in discussions, it is time consuming to give students feedback. However, you do not need to write a master's thesis to get the point across. I have seen so many faculty members provide paragraphs of feedback and I bet the students stop reading after a few sentences. There's an ideal point that's just right, and you need to learn how to find that. Regardless of it taking extra time, you should feel obligated to provide some rationale for the grade a student receives.

I will give you an out, though. If you have three things to grade in a week—let's say discussion, a short reading reflection, and a small project, I can't expect you to give specific feedback on every grade. I would say 2 out of the 3. It's easier to grade and provide 'sort of' feedback if you use a rubric and the LMS has a rubric grader built in (Canvas and Blackboard do, as of now). Papers should always have feedback. Discussion is important in the first few weeks of class until the students have a good idea of what they need to do to get full credit. If they lose points after that, and your grading criteria are very clear, and your grading consistent, then sometimes it would be ok to just grade if you have other things that need your feedback attention.

The sandwich method:

If you're still wondering what ice cream has to do with it, I will explain a little further than I did in the first paragraph. The top cookie and bottom cookie need to be positive (because the cookie is better than the ice cream, don't you think?) and the ice cream in the middle is the feedback that gives the student the more direct, possibly undesirable information. Sometimes this is hard to do. Sometimes the student work is so horrible that it's impossible to find something positive to say, but I strongly encourage you to find something, even if it's "Thank you, Mary, for submitting your paper. It was great to read your perspective."★ That is usually my go-to if a student's paper just really bombed. I follow it with what went wrong and then I end it with something nice again such as, "I look forward to reading what you turn in next week. Shoot for those full points!"

You don't want to make the student feel horrible, but you do want to say just enough so he understands what needs to be done next time, even if you say, "It would be helpful to re-review the assignment guidelines to improve your grade." This is why having a rubric can decrease what you have to type. You highlight the student's performance areas, and then provide an additional sentence or two. I try my best to avoid using 'You' in a negative way. So, instead of saying, "You did not follow directions", I might say what you read a short while ago. It's passive voice, but it usually softens the blow of feedback they won't want to read.

When a student deserves praise, by golly, praise them!★ You probably enjoy hearing compliments, and students do too. Even if they were awful at grammar and punctuation, maybe their content was original and thought provoking. If so, don't forget what's positive even if the negative overshadowed it. When I grade student discussions and I have students who just go way beyond my expectations, I tell them! I might say, 'Wow, Mark, you were a discussion rock star this week! Keep it up!" Or, "Helen, your participation this week was stellar. Thanks for being such an excellent example for your peers!" This praise makes the students feel great and does encourage them to keep up their over-achieving and there's nothing wrong with that!

Speaking of grading discussion, I don't give extensive feedback a great deal of the time. Just two or three sentences will do. Remember when I said keep a file of feedback? That's what you should do for your discussions as well as for your assignments. After you are comfortable with an assignment and know you will be using it again, save feedback for an A performance, B, C, D, and F (I know I am repeating myself, but it's done on purpose). The comments will likely be similar, but you might have to personalize it at times. Certainly for the A and the F you can keep the feedback generic. This will save you a lot of time.

Grading papers:

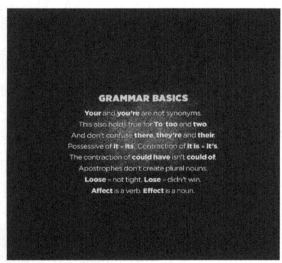

GRAMMAR BASICS

Your and **you're** are not synonyms.
This also holds true for **To, too** and **two**.
And don't confuse **there, they're** and **their**.
Possessive of **it** = **its**. Contraction of **it is** = **it's**.
The contraction of **could have** isn't **could of**.
Apostrophes don't create plural nouns.
Loose = not tight. **Lose** = didn't win.
Affect is a verb. **Effect** is a noun.

B. Jordan / Flickr

When it comes to grading papers, you need to do some soul searching. Many times people who teach English can't help themselves. They have the "red pen mentality". They feel this unavoidable urge to print the paper, pull out a red pen, and mark each comma splice, tense error, and sentence fragment. Please try to avoid this. I am speaking to you as a rehabilitated 'red pen' junkie. Well, I didn't use red, but I did use green or purple! I realized that correcting the errors really didn't help my students. I think you should tell them if they consistently have errors like run-ons, comma splices, and fragments. Show them a few examples of them. Then, tell them to find the others on their own. Maybe you can even give them a few points extra credit if they fix the errors they find on their own!★ It's a great way to reinforce a new skill and their ability to recognize the errors.

This can work for any type of teaching. Sometimes we English teachers spend too much time looking for these little things that we miss the content entirely. We might have a brilliant thinker who can't spell worth a you-know-what and all we're focused on is that. Sure, students need to learn how to write in grammatically correct sentences, and need to learn how to logically frame their thoughts, but do not ignore the ideas and perspectives.

Peer review helps:

Do you want to know a trade secret? It's not a secret to those who have taught writing in online classes for a while—and that is that peer review is incredibly valuable★. I will argue until I am blue in the face that it is not as valuable face-to-face. The online environment is nearly anonymous. Students generally do not know each other and because of that, and because they don't have to look at each other in the eyes the following Thursday, they will be honest, even brutally so. I assign peer review often in my online classes, even those that are not writing-based. If a project is coming due, instead of having a discussion, I will have a peer review. There are methods to doing this well, though.

First, you cannot expect students to know what to say when they looks at someone else's work. Some of them will be very leery of it. So, to ease that anxiety, you provide the prompts for the review. Give them a list of questions to answer, or things to look for. Here are two examples:

Post your letter to the media that's due this week. Even if it's not complete, post what you have by THURSDAY.

Then, choose TWO students and evaluate their letter using the following questions.

1. *What is the purpose of this letter?*
2. *What was your response to the initial paragraph? How did you feel after you read it?*
3. *What is the overall tone of the letter?*
4. *What's the overall message of the letter?*
5. *What comments do you have about the letter?*
6. *Any suggestions for improvement or revision?*

This week you should be working on your brochure for employees about the country in which you'll soon be working. Please attach a copy of what you have by THURSDAY. Peer reviews are due no later than SATURDAY.

Then, choose TWO students and evaluate their brochures. Please use the following questions in your review.

1. *What is the overall visual impression of the brochure?*
2. *Is information laid out effectively and images used appropriately?*
3. *What is the general message you received from this brochure?*
4. *What persuasive strategies were used (see chapter 11)?*
5. *Would you be persuaded to move to this country after receiving this brochure? Explain your answer and offer any other suggestions.*

A good practice for you would be to review the rubric or grading criteria and then write the questions that guide their review based upon what you're looking for★. This will help the students analyze other writings better, as well as help you in the long run get higher quality assignments.

I assign more points on peer review weeks than regular discussion weeks and students will lose points if they don't answer every question or provide constructive feedback. I do not want to see "good job. I liked that" or "wow, you are a good writer. I have no suggestions." That does not fly with me. I have found that my older students and students who are in the military provide the best peer reviews. What I do is have the students share a draft of their paper/project/assignment generally on Thursdays. Since their assignments are due on Sundays, I ask them to complete 2 or 3 peer reviews by Saturday. I might assign 2 if it's a small(ish) class, if they're freshman, or the assignment is complex. I might assign 3 if it's a short(er) paper, the class is a bit larger (to make sure everyone gets at least 1 review, if not 2), or if the class is a higher level. I do not participate in peer review discussions.

What's nice is that you can be almost assured that the work you get on Sunday is better if a peer review is involved than if it isn't. I can give you a great example. For the Business Communication & Writing class the students were supposed to write a letter to their (pretend) employees trying to convince them to move overseas. One student must have misunderstood the assignment because what she wrote was not at all what she should have. Her first peer reviewer told her this and saved that student from certain doom! That's overly dramatic, but I'm sure it saved her from significant stress.

Peer review also helps give students confidence in their own abilities to recognize quality writing. When I taught face to face I told my students something like this,

> *"I know you're in a beginning writing class, but that doesn't mean you're bad writers. It means that you're learning. However, your brain instinctively knows good writing. You know when you read something well written versus something poorly written, don't you? You might not know what's wrong exactly, but something's wrong. If you sense something's not right, just indicate that on the student's paper with maybe a question mark or a 'I think something's not right here'."*

You can say the same things online. I will remind them if they stumble while reading, or if they have to go back and re-read a sentence because it's not making sense, then that's their brain's way of telling them that something's amiss. So, indicate that to the student who wrote the paper. You don't need to know how to fix it, but just tell them where you stumbled. Students need to feel empowered and the peer reviews save you time in the long run.

While I digressed for a while on peer review (I feel that strongly about it), it does relate to feedback as it's the matter of students providing each other with feedback that will hopefully lead to the students getting better feedback from you once they turn in their papers. Whatever you can do to help your students help themselves, the easier your job will be and the more meaningful the collaboration between the students.

Chapter 11 checklist: Feedback

- Sandwich the negative feedback between to positive things
- Praise students when they deserve it! Do it often!
- Try not to give in to the urge to download, print papers, and mark on them
- Use peer review in lieu of weekly discussion
- The student work you get after peer review is better than work you'd get without peer review
- Peer review increases student confidence in their own abilities
- Empower students to know good writing when they see it!
- Consider contacting the top 3-5 students in your course at the end and giving them a virtual high-five for an awesome job!

12

Growing pains

I don't know about you, but I'm a perfectionist when it comes to anything I create, attempt, design, or do. I do not like the feeling of being a fish out of water. I will do everything I can to avoid floundering around gasping and freaking out. It's a difficult lesson at times for me personally, but I am not perfect and everything I do will not be perfect the first time around. This is true for you as well. You can go through training, and read about "best practices" (did I say I hate this term yet? If I haven't, I will say it now. I hate this term and do not use it- yes, I used it now, but just to tell you that I don't like it). Why? Ok, let me tell you. I think it's horrible because who says they're the 'best'? And, do they always remain the 'best'? In what circumstances are they the 'best'? Don't let me keep going…

Finding EFFECTIVE practices is a good habit and when you do read about something that someone else has done that worked well for them, be sure to save it. I will reiterate that you should get yourself in the habit of saving sites that are useful by using a digital repository for your saved sites (Diigo is my favorite right now). So, you've adequately prepared yourself, so the course should be wonderful, right? Um… sometimes.

A. Arthur / Flickr

Occasionally it's wonderful, the students love it, you figure out what you're doing quickly, you find a rhythm that works for you, and you feel fabulous after your first online course. This is not the rule, my friends; it's the exception. Please be prepared that some things might go wrong. It doesn't mean you suck at this online stuff, and does not mean you should throw in the towel and bad mouth online in your department and potentially to the universe. It just means you figure out what didn't work like you thought, get out your virtual tool belt, and try to fix it. I will argue with anyone that it takes a good three times before you really get the course how you want it to be and even after that you might still revise some things.

Before I give you a list of what could go wrong and potentially how to avoid it, I want to give you a qualification. What I am about to share is for an average-sized online course—about 25 students. If you have a small course (15 students or less) or a large course (over 30 students), you will have a different set of possible things that could go awry. Go back to Chapter 10 for specifics about small and large courses.

Potential issues and avoidance tactics:

1. *Your dates, assignments, expectations, and/or other things aren't consistent.* I have had this happen more than once and it's not fun at all. Sometimes you change something at the last minute on the course schedule/calendar and then you forgot to change the date in the assignment, and in the weekly agenda. Or, you say you expect them to participate 3 days a week in the syllabus, but say 2 days a week elsewhere.

How to avoid this:

- Avoid entering dates anywhere in your course until you're completely done designing. Use due DAYS instead. For example, discussion posts due on Thursday, at least one reply by Friday, reading reflection due Sunday.

- ONLY put specific due dates on one document. I like course calendars/schedules that students can download and print. This way if you have to modify due dates you're only modifying that document. I do not recommend setting specific due dates for assignments using the LMS assignment tool. If you don't want students turning in work late, then tell them and if they try it, they deal with the consequences. Only put these in the syllabus if you're required to do so.

- Have someone proof your course. This someone should not be you. Ask them to specifically look at what's due and when in order to make sure all content matches.

2. *Your students are appearing to be disengaged in the course during the first week.* I can't think of something more disheartening than having your students appear to be disinterested in your class and you wondering where everyone is when the first week is nearly over.

How to avoid this:

- Make sure you send a welcome announcement to the students a week or so before the class begins. Give them warm fuzzies. Encourage them to start right away, as soon as they have access to the class.

- Have an introductions forum that goes beyond "tell us a little about yourself". Play a game. Encourage them to share with each other and for goodness sakes, participate in this forum as often as you can the first week! If you're present they will feel it and participate more.

- Make sure that you have clear requirements for participation and these requirements are understood so they know what to expect. A syllabus quiz will help this as well as a little reminder from you in advance.

- Personally contact each student that has not participated the first 5 days of the class. Honestly, those students will typically fail or withdraw, that's my experience; however, you can do your best to draw them in with a personal email or phone call. I like to say, "Did you forget about us?" and keep it lighthearted, but filled with gentle warning.

3. *Students are not participating in discussions as much as you'd hoped.* This does happen sometimes, and generally that's a result of a few things.

How to avoid this:

- One, make sure you have sufficient motivation for them to participate. Is it worth enough points? 15 to 20% is ideal. Do they know how much participation is worth? They should!

- Do they know what's expected in terms of participation? Be sure it's very clear and if it's not, then that could explain it. Spell it out- how many days, how many posts, and the post length requirement (or general guidelines of what's acceptable).

4. *You realize that you've assigned way too much work.* You're overwhelmed and so are they. This is usually a result of inexperienced online instructors and those who overcompensate for the lack of face-to-face time with more work.

How to avoid this:

This is a tricky one. You've already created a syllabus; you already have a whole course planned out. This does not mean that you should leave it at is and freak everyone out, including yourself. What you can do in this situation is do a quick review of the upcoming weeks.

- See what you can cut out without affecting your learning objectives. It could be requiring less in terms of number of posts or peer replies.

- It could be decreasing the page requirement of upcoming papers. You could cut out a few quizzes if you have them, or take out some test questions.

- Make sure that you make the changes all at once if possible. Then, fix the syllabus or course schedule and then the course content.

- Email the students with the changes and an explanation of why you've decided to change things. They will understand, I promise.

One of the best ways to avoid this is to have an experienced instructional designer or online instructor review your course in advance. This person should be able to tell if you've required too much. Remember, no more than two graded assignments that you have to grade yourself each week. This is one major reason why it's so important to have your course completely designed before it's taught.

Chapter 12 checklist: Sometimes things happen

- Please stop using the term 'best practices'
- Make sure and save effective practices and good resources when you find them. Use Diigo or Evernote. They're great
- Do not expect your first online teaching experience to be all blissful and lovely
- It takes several times to get it working like a well-oiled machine
- Have someone objective review your course before it's live to check for consistent language, broken links, and ease of navigation
- Be sure to review the issues and avoidance tactics in the chapter

13

Just getting your feet wet

Getting started with blended learning:

K. Tegtmeyer / Flickr

There's this interesting myth that seems to be prolific in the academy, and that myth is that blended, or hybrid teaching is somehow a 'stepping stone' to fully online teaching. I completely disagree with this and want to tell you that it is indeed a myth. Starting with hybrid before going fully online is not 'getting your feet wet', that is, not if the water you're dipping your feet into leads into the lake of online learning. If we were talking about one thing leading to another, it is my belief that blended learning is something someone ought to do after they've dived in the water, swam around until they were getting weary, then jumped out, toweled off, sat in the sun to reflect a little, and became re-energized. Blended teaching is not easy and should not be seen as a natural start for someone who's leery of fully online.

I will strongly suggest that to have the best preparation for quality hybrid teaching you should be experienced as a face-to-face and online teacher, then have your own hybrid learning experience that immerses you in the environment you are expected to emulate for your own course. If that's not possible or available, a more natural stepping stone is to have a tech-enhanced course—a course where you put a lot of your content online, you require online discussions outside of class, have students submit assignments and receive grades and feedback online, so you have practice thinking about what goes online and what goes on in the classroom.

I know people will argue with me on this point and that's ok. I believe this to be true because blended course design requires you to compartmentalize, contextualize your course in two ways, not just one. For fully online you're only focused on one environment—the virtual one. For a blended course you have to focus on that AND what you're going to

104

do F2F (face-to-face). Therefore, if you've never taught online you do not have a good idea or grasp of what it's like, what works, what doesn't, and how much time it might take for students to grasp the concepts they need to learn and apply. You'll be playing a guessing game there.

If you've taught online before, then you totally understand how the online portion will go- you will have experience that has told you what might work best F2F so you can naturally make that split in your course activities with confidence. It's the splitting of the course that makes it more difficult because it means the students are also splitting their learning and you are splitting your teaching. It could be a big mess if you don't know what you're doing.

I will not tell you that it can't be done with someone inexperienced online, because I know it has been done and maybe even done well. I'm just discouraging it and suggesting that blended experiences wait a bit until the online course has been taught a few times as it will be a lot easier on the instructor and the students★.

When planning your blended course your focus needs to be on your course outcomes first and foremost, and then continue having them as the focus throughout the design process. This is almost identical to what I suggested for a fully online course, isn't it? That's because outcomes and objectives are the root of your course. You want them strong and sturdy—supported by the solid branches of the course content. Start at the end. What should the students know by the end of the class? What should they be able to do? Work backwards and create weekly objectives from the course-level outcomes★ .

How well do you like yours blended?

Once you have the weekly objectives (that are written in measurable, observable terms that are tied into the course outcomes), figure out what kind of blended you're going to have. Your institution might mandate this for you like a 50/50 split; half the time you're online, the other F2F. They could mandate this, by the way, but you might have the freedom to decide how that's done. Maybe you meet F2F once a week and the other day is covered online—or, you could meet one week online, one week F2F. Find out what your options are to figure out what you can do. Perhaps how much you're F2F is up to you.

Keep the 'how often' in the back of your mind when designing. I wouldn't suggest deciding this in advance unless you don't get the choice. You want the activity to determine the best environment, not the environment deciding the activity★. Design the class as if it were totally online, at least

Cookbookman17 / Flickr

at first. Put all of your content online (please do not give the students handouts because you're F2F... not only is that a bad choice environmentally, it's also a reflection that you're still holding on to 'old school' habits).

Face to face time is crucial:

Your F2F time must be meaningful. It must make sense to the students because they will wonder why they have the inconvenience of traveling- so make that time worth it. You do not use it to lecture★. You can give them online lectures (short ones), instructor notes, or instructional videos online. They don't need to see you to 'hear' what you have to say. Use the F2F time to DO things. Discussion? Probably not, that's better online, although activity with discussion/reflection is a good thing face to face. It could be time for small group work, debates, creating things, student-led teaching moments, lab work, experiments, or other active learning techniques★.

Even though you will meet F2F, you can require that readings, viewing of lectures or videos be complete before they come to class. That 'flipped' approach will provide your students with sufficient background to guide what they're doing with you and each other during that F2F time. Further, even though you're meeting F2F, you can continue the discussion or reflection online for the rest of the week.

What you do online is important too:

I will take a moment here to vent. It bothers me to read research that describes hybrid teaching as "some F2F time with the instructor with the rest of the course being done in a computer-mediated environment".

106

Too often instructors who design hybrid courses assume that their work, their personal work, is only done face to face and while the students are learning online they do not participate. This is awful, wrong, and a disservice to students. The online portion of the class should continue the development of the learning community, and that cannot happen if the students are left to read material, take quizzes, and post assignments. There are a few conceptual frameworks for quality blended learning such as Picciano (2009) and Shea (2007), both of which insist that learning requires social presence and teaching presence. Thus, do not leave your students to their own devices for the online portions of your course.

Students should interact F2F and online; they should be regularly discussing and collaborating. Your presence is as important in the class with walls as it is in the class without them. Creating a high quality hybrid course is a challenge, but when it is done well, learning that happens can exceed the learning that happens in fully online courses and traditional courses. However, instructors need to learn how to do it well if they wish for their students to have the most significant learning experience possible for their course.

It needs to be connected and make sense:

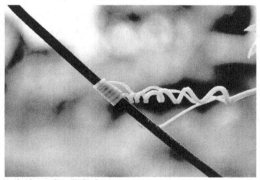

Whologwhy / Flickr

One of the important aspects of blended learning that's missed by some instructors is that connection between everything in the course—what's done online must relate to what's done F2F and that connection needs to be continual, pretty much seamless.

Be sure that those connections are clear when you design your course. Students will not be happy if you create a "course and a half", meaning they have a fully online course that's sufficient to meet the outcomes, but you want another half of a course F2F just because. There is research to support what I am saying about the students as well as what I am saying about the complexity of the hybrid environment. I promised I wouldn't fill this book with research citations, so Google the topic in Scholar and you'll see what I mean.

In your design try to avoid the tendency to over assign work to your students. This happens mostly with inexperienced online instructors because they feel like more work needs to compensate for the loss of the other F2F day. This is why having the course designed like it was fully online helps a lot. In a fully online course you'd assign no more than 3 graded things each week—ideally, 2.

If you have F2F time maybe you only have one online discussion question each week- maybe you only require one peer post instead of 2 or 3 if it were fully online. Be mindful of the amount of reading and watching too. Write a weekly agenda just like you would for an online class and be honest with yourself when you see the 'to do' list or ask a peer whether or not the workload is acceptable★.

Using the "A" word again:

You need to know how you're going to assess the in-class time. Will there be a grade for attendance for F2F time? If not, how will they be motivated to attend? Perhaps some sort of policy should be clear in the syllabus about that. Please try to avoid having them hand you anything during F2F time. If you have them do an activity such as an in-class presentation, do your grading online- give them an electronic rubric or something of that nature. One benefit of online is that everything can be traced and viewed—nothing's lost in terms of grading, feedback, or the like. In situations of grade review or student complaints, this will go a long way to protect you; plus, it's very traditional, everything that blended learning isn't. Try to stick with the innovation theme even though you might not be used to it.

Be sure that your schedule is available well in advance and that it contains specific dates on it with your F2F meetings★. No need to say that certain things are "online", as that should be understood. Do not put dates anywhere else in the class except for that one document. In your weekly agendas you can list F2F meetings, but just put, for example: "Monday, in-class meeting 3-4:30pm in Room 102". This way you can avoid modifying dates★. Even better you can just say: In-class meeting scheduled this week: see schedule for date/time/location!

There's a lot to learn when it comes to the blended environment. Like online, it too can be overwhelming and sometimes frustrating. Finding help online would likely be something useful for you, especially if you search for blended samples of your course subject. You might find some fantastic ideas that someone else shared. In terms of resources for general design, Simmons College has a great resource page for those wanting to design a blended course. Visit the page to find a sample redesign schedule, different checklists and templates: http://at.simmons.edu/blendedlearning/implement/simmons.php

It would be ideal if your institution offered preparation or development for those who wish to teach hybrid courses. I know from direct experience that it is not common, at least not yet. It would be ideal for the institution to have an instructional design expert who is very familiar with hybrid learning environments that you could consult while designing your course. If you have this, then consider yourself very fortunate and use it to its greatest potential! Seeking help is not an admittance of stupidity or lack of knowledge; it is a smart move because you can always learn something new.

I would like to encourage all institutions that want to expand their hybrid offerings to first secure adequate preparation and resources for the faculty members who will explore this method. It is easy to 'mess up', so take the time to get it done right the first time. If you do not have access to institutional training, support, workshops, or staff to help, then seek it on your own. Many workshops are available out there—and I know for certain The Online Learning Consortium offers a blended learning series, at least at the time I'm writing this book.

I will repeat here that blended is not easy, and you need to give yourself a break if things don't go that well at first. It will likely take 3 times before it feels like it's working—the same is true for a fully online class★. Take careful note of what worked and what needed refinement so that when it is time to revise, you did not forget. I suggest electronic notes (I use Evernote). It will be helpful for you to get some formative feedback from the students during the course too. Maybe give them a quick anonymous survey about mid way through the class, or even 1/3 into it so you can get their honest opinions about the F2F and online portions of the course★.

Inevitably, you will revise the class more than once—it's just to be expected. Hopefully you'll learn some good lessons on this blended journey and if you do, share them. The academic community needs people to share their triumphs and their failures! You can help other people, even if it might be a little humbling to do so at times. If you can, offer to do a workshop at your institution. Even if you're nowhere near an expert, you can empower others to give it a try too. If you are willing, research your adventure because significant research is seriously lacking for hybrid teaching and what a quality hybrid course looks like. Good luck!

Chapter 13 checklist: Hybrid/Blended

- o Hybrid is the same as blended teaching
- o Blended is not easier than online and is not a natural step towards it
- o Teachers who delve into blended should be experienced online first
- o Start planning blended just like online: with outcomes and objectives first
- o Know what your blend will look like in advance
- o Face-to-face time is critical- make it worth their while
- o Just because you're blended does not excuse you from participating online
- o What you do online and F2F needs to be seamlessly connected
- o Do not make this a course and a half because it's blended
- o Know how to assess your F2F time
- o Give yourself a break; it won't be perfect the first time

14

Ok, what now?

I hope you've been able to learn a great deal about online teaching, from getting started conceptualizing an online course, getting your hands dirty in the LMS putting your new knowledge to work designing, and how to make it all work once the course is filled with eager (and sometimes not-so-eager) students. It's also my hope that even if you have some experience teaching online already that you've taken some new tidbits from this book that make your time and investment worth it.

Overall, the most important thing I want you to remember is:

Online Teaching Is Not Easy.

The next most important thing is that quality needs to be part of the equation. Students deserve more than readings, assignments, and feedback online. They deserve the highest quality courses that you can

design and teach, and I wrote this book to encourage that quality regardless of where, what grade, or what course you're teaching.

Hurray for online learning centers:

The quality focus and assessment usually comes from a department who oversees online courses and instructional design. It's my hope you have a place like this, but it's surprising to me that many places still don't.

Maybe at those places there's no one particularly in charge of online learning. Maybe it's still like Tombstone and the online teachers are non-criminal outlaws doing what they want how they want, and without a good Sheriff in town, that will continue. Talk to people who can make decisions and make sure that you have someone in charge of online learning. This is imperative to quality courses and programming.

Sometimes this happens in the Center for Teaching and Learning (and the dozens of other acronyms and words that stand for this same thing); I would like to see institutions follow those who have very successful online programs and create their own centers for online learning or distance education (but I dislike using the word 'distance', just personal opinion). I've seen better work come out of institutions that devote a specific center, specific resources, and specific people to the online initiatives without spreading them thinly to cover all teaching and learning efforts.

While good teaching is good teaching, online or face-to-face, keeping focused on one delivery method will help the institution in the long run. I think the two centers should collaborate because skills do overlap, especially the use of technology. I also know for a fact that those who teach online do end up becoming better face-to-face teachers, so the relationship is indeed there. People who lead teaching and learning centers should have the focus on the in-class people, and thus those who work there should have specific qualifications and merit to do so. Likewise, those who lead online learning centers should also have very specific qualifications, experience, and skills.

Ideally you are able to consult with a center for online learning when you need training or instructional design assistance. If you do not, then you will need to do some of this work all on your own or seek the assistance of others outside of your institution. Some mistakes I have seen in staffing these centers is using people who do not have enough experience teaching online, do not have any or not enough experience designing online courses, and do not have the right people skills to influence faculty and administrators.

Progress can be slowed or not happen at all if the right people are not in the right positions when it comes to leading an area of higher education that is constantly changing. If you don't have a center yet, consider sharing this information with the people in charge so that they consider creating one and take serious time deciding who should staff it. Usually one administrator, one instructional designer, an instructional technologist, and a program manager/office manager would be a good start.

What about you, though?

When it comes to your own efforts to design your own online course, you need to be sure to give yourself enough time. If I am held down to the wire I can get an 8-week online course designed in less than a month, but it's not an ideal situation. I believe you can get a complete, full-semester course designed over the summer if you dedicate time to it every single week, maybe a total of 10 hours a week or so. The amount of time you spend designing is going to vary extensively based on a lot of things.

It will take less time if your institution has an online course 'shell' that has a pre-designed skeleton of a course that you fill in with your own content. I do that for my institution and it really helps faculty. It doesn't limit them, but provides locations for all course content. I even have images in the lessons that are generic enough to be re-used (or they can change them). If you have an instructional designer, maybe this person can do this for faculty at your institution too. If you don't, then consider the time it will take to get the skeleton of the course ready before it's time to load content.

For a first-time course designer it can take up to a year to get the course ready to go, especially if you have a large teaching and research load, a family, and other responsibilities. I think that you should limit yourself to 6 months and set monthly goals to get specific portions completed★. Set a time frame and stick to it. Remind yourself and stick to it even when you feel like you're too busy. It's best to keep notes while you're designing too, just in case you think of things as you're going along but don't have time to actually "do" it★.

If possible, have someone help you review your course. If you don't have anyone in-house, that might be challenging since most institutions will not give outsiders access to the LMS. Hopefully there's someone who can periodically review what you're doing to give you feedback. Speaking of, sometimes it's hard to put yourself out there like that, to do something in which you're not too confident to begin with, and then show it to someone who will judge you. I don't like being put in that position, and perhaps most people don't, but it's necessary for you to do the best you can. Do not wait until the course is almost done before you get feedback; that could be devastating for you★.

While designing be sure to have ONE quality metric on hand that you use to check yourself★. Pick whatever one you think is best for you or, of course, pick the one your institution suggests. It might be a QM institution and if that's the case, be sure you have that rubric so you can mark off items as you create them to self-assess. I don't think one metric is better than any other. For me, I like making my own because mine are an amalgamation of all of them and a few aspects I personally believe are important. You really can't go wrong with a quality metric for online course design as long as it is one that's widely used or one that a qualified individual created for your institution.

This can be an emotional experience:

More than likely you will go through a slew of emotions as you design and teach online so be prepared for that. There will be moments of frustration that might put your computer's safety in jeopardy, as well as moments of brilliance when you come up with something ingenious for your students to do. Let your family know what you're doing so that when you're locked in your office, the bedroom, or the bathroom that they can give you the time you need to focus for a few hours★.

R.J. Fox / Flickr

One of the biggest mistakes we academics make is that we want our educational and academic endeavors to be perfect the first time. Please listen to me that your course will not be perfect the first time because you need to teach it a few times before you get a sense for how all of your course pieces work together. Realizing that something just doesn't work is totally normal; doing a complete revision of several weeks or major assignments is normal too. This is a learning process for you and a process of transformation.

In addition, each group of students will vary. One group might struggle with an assignment and the next semester's students might find it too easy. Take notes while teaching so you know what you're thinking about everything. Give yourself ideas for the future, but do not jump to making drastic changes based on ONE online class. Little changes, sure, fix those as you go, but big things, hold off and just take note of them★.

Making changes:

I do not suggest that you take the break between fall and spring to make any major change to your online course★. It is tempting, though, especially if you're teaching it again right away. What happens sometimes is you jump the gun to make a big change, but forget the other things that mention the previous assignment or activity or you later remember why you had it that way in the first place and then you're in a big, sour pickle.

Give yourself a few months to make a revision of your online course and once you do, have someone else review the class and look for inconsistencies. What happens so often is you decide you need to change due dates of assignments, adjust the requirements of an assignment, or remove an assignment completely and in the process of making those changes you forget that you also mention these in the lesson, you have an assignment link to delete, and a handout to modify too. Inconsistencies in your course will frustrate your students and you don't want to do that.

Like I mentioned previously, if you need to make tiny, innocuous adjustments, that's fine after you teach a class one time. If you're thinking that you need to revise something, wait until you've taught the course twice just to see if having a different class makes a difference. Be patient and observant. Gather feedback from your students, too, if you're questioning what you've designed. They will probably be honest with you if you ask for feedback.

What do the students think?

Some institutions do not have electronic student evaluations, and in these circumstances it is difficult to get reliable data about the learning experience. If you don't have electronic evaluations, then you should create a short survey for your students that you use for your own purposes of revising and learning what you did well and what you can do to improve. If you're teaching online for the first time, consider a very short survey during maybe week 4 or 5 to ask them how the course is going, how you're doing as the instructor, etc. Ask very specific questions like, "How is the course pace for you? (too difficult, just right, too easy)" or "How responsive am I to your questions and concerns?" And "How is my course participation?" You can do this free through online survey tools. Google "free survey tool" and see what you find.

If you do get an electronic evaluation, hopefully it's appropriate for an online class. I've seen departments make an electronic version of the face-to-face evaluation and some of the questions are not applicable and very important questions are not asked that relate to the specifics of the online environment. The student comments and responses should be useful for you when it comes to seeing the big picture of the course.

Keep learning, experimenting, and sharing!

Teaching online can be a very fulfilling experience that just keeps on changing. I love it! It gives you opportunities to be creative and you have so many tools to use! In order to "be in the know", make sure you keep yourself up-to-date about what's going on in the field, what others are doing, and read the research. There are many resources out there to help you in this endeavor. I mentioned several of them in a previous chapter.

C. Maya / Flickr

Your online class should be a fluid thing and you should feel the need to improve as often as you can, which might be a new approach that you read in someone's anecdotal article or it could be a new tool you saw mentioned on Twitter. You should definitely consider writing your own articles about your experiences or do research to add to the literature. We need quality research to inform our practice.

Please share with the academic community and share with your own community within your institution. I know I am repeating myself again because I have mentioned the importance of sharing your new learning with other people. Sometimes faculty get bored with the same old workshops from the same old people so much that the emails end up getting ignored. If you, another faculty member, offer to share and teach them something new, the novelty might bring them to you. You don't have to be face to face, either; consider offering a virtual workshop. Be risky; be different, and encourage others to try something new.

Concluding thoughts:

People who design courses and teach online are a sub civilization of the academic culture. These people who embrace the environment have the potential to influence others to join in, and the awareness about what works well in instructional design and how to effectively teach online positively affects other aspects of teaching. When many people start experiencing this, a culture shift starts to happen campus-wide. It's powerful, transformational, but fragile.

The faculty is the backbone of a successful online initiative and that should always be the institutional focus. Faculty members need to be supported through these processes and without that support, confidence and motivation can falter. Some of them are self-motivated and will innovate for their own reasons while others need a lot of encouragement and handholding. Ideally someone will be there to serve that purpose. I do not believe that course design should be outsourced, nor do I believe that textbook publisher websites should take the place of an instructor-designed online course (despite the publishers having way more money to do eye-popping, sexy things with the material). Faculty should design and faculty should teach. Period.

I have given you more opinions than you've asked for, stood on my soapbox so many times that I got a lower body workout while writing this book, and I've spilled my treasure trove of tips and hard-learned lessons, all of this so you keep your mind intact while becoming a stellar online designer and educator! I welcome your comments, suggestions, and tips and look forward to hearing about your own online victories!

Chapter 14 checklist: Final thoughts

- Online teaching is not easy and don't let someone who doesn't know convince you otherwise
- Consult your center for teaching and learning if you do not have a center for distance/online learning
- Give yourself enough time to do this right; don't rush it unless you have to
- See if your institution has a course shell to use to minimize design time
- Have someone help you by reviewing your course, preferably 2 people- one from your discipline and one not
- Use a quality metric while designing, whether it's external from your institution or institutionally designed or vetted
- Be prepared for moments of sheer brilliance and frustration!
- Revise the course after it's over and give it two times before you make drastic changes
- Make sure you have an electronic evaluation and, if not, seek student feedback through other means
- Share your experiences at conferences and through writing! We need you!

Acknowledgements

I am infinitely grateful for the advice and counsel of the following friends and colleagues who graciously volunteered their time to review this book. I hope to return the favor one day.

Dr. Curt Bonk, Indiana University

Dr. Shannon Burton, Michigan State University

Lauren Edgell, Millersville University

Tammy Powell, Kennesaw State University

Dr. Larry Ragan, Penn State University

Dr. Jason Rhode, Northern Illinois University

Dr. Brian Udermann, University of Wisconsin-LaCrosse

Dr. Jean-Marc Wise, Florida State University

I would also like to thank Ryan Shelton, the women's basketball coach at IU Northwest, for his brilliance and generosity in designing the cover of this book.

Book's cover photo:

jmiltenburg. (Photographer). (2013, September 20). *apple and books* [digital image]. Retrieved from http://morguefile.com/archive/#/?q=apple&sort=pop&photo_lib=morgueFile

Other images in the book were found on Flickr using a Creative Commons/Commercial use allowed license. Some are from Morguefile, all of which have this distinction. Images are cited anyway, both under the image and on the Image credits page; you can never be too careful with copyright

About the Author

Dr. Angela Velez-Solic is the Associate Director for the Center for Innovation and Scholarship in Teaching and Learning at Indiana University Northwest. She also serves as a Clinical Assistant Professor of Education for IUN. She has been teaching at the college level since 1998, mostly courses in English, Humanities, and Communication. She began teaching online in 2005 and quickly became immersed in the teaching environment and fascinated with preparing faculty to teach online and supporting faculty teaching from a distance.

In 2007 she made a career move into faculty development, support, and training and in 2009 added administrative duties to her repertoire. She enjoys helping transform hesitant faculty and campuses that are "late to the online game". She is also an expert faculty trainer, a skilled instructional designer, and master online teacher. At the time of this publication, she has trained upwards of 700 faculty members around the world to teach online!

Besides her academic and professional work she enjoys spending time with her 4 children, 3 stepchildren, and husband in Northwest Indiana while dreaming about living in the mountains of Southwest Virginia (one day). Find out more on her website: justcallmeang.com, on Twitter: @JustCallMeAngVS and LinkedIn.

References

Berry, R.W. (2009). Meeting the challenges of teaching large online classes: Shifting to a learner-focus. *Journal of Online Learning and Teaching*, 5(1). Retrieved on June 17, 2014 from http://jolt.merlot.org/vol5no1/berry_0309.htm

Parra, J.L. (2010). *A multiple-case study on the impact of teacher professional development for online teaching on face-to-face classroom teaching practices.* (Doctoral Dissertation). Retrieved from ProQuest Dissertations and Theses. (Accession Order No: AAT 3397778).

Picciano, A.G. (2009). Blending with purpose: The multimodal model. *Journal of the Research Center for Educational Technology*, 5(1). Kent, OH: Kent State University.

Shea, P. (2007). Towards a conceptual framework for learning in blended environments. In A. G. Picciano & C. D. Dziuban (Eds.), *Blended learning: Research perspectives*. Needham, MA: Sloan Consortium. pp. 19-35.

Velez-Solic, A. & Kilibarda, V. (2015). Factors that contribute to transformation of faculty after an online training course. Submitted for review to an academic journal at the time of this publication.

Weimer, M. (2015). Effective ways to structure discussion. *Faculty Focus*. Retrieved from http://www.facultyfocus.com/articles/teaching-professor-blog/effective-ways-structure-discussion/

Image Credits

Amy. (Photographer). (2010, March 2). *Post-it Motivation* [digital image]. Retrieved from http://bit.ly/1scMhlk

Arthur, A. (Photographer). (2010, July 11). *Tree Grown Over Rock* [digital image]. Retrieved from https://www.flickr.com/photos/andyarthur/5529790296/in/photolist

Bamford, D. (Photographer). (2012, February 18). *authentic* [digital image]. Retrieved from http://bit.ly/1G9MUlW

Black, M. (Photographer). (2010, November 29). Eggroll [digital image]. Retrieved from https://www.flickr.com/photos/mackenzieblack/5235085338/in/photolist

Brekke, D. (Photographer). (2006, October 22). *Play-Doh* [digital image]. Retrieved from http://bit.ly/160doLU

'Campbell, S. (Photographer). (2008, November 5). *Pencil and eraser on paper* [digital image]. Retrieved from http://bit.ly/12EKoXV

Christian, C. (Photographer). (2012, February 16). *You Are What You Create* [digital image]. Retrieved from http://bit.ly/1w60aH3

Cookbookman17. (Photographer). (2011, August 24). *Blender* [digital image]. Retrieved from http://bit.ly/1vFx69v

Daily, R. (Photographer). (2012, July 20). *Ice Cream Sandwich* [digital image]. Retrieved from http://bit.ly/1z0bJzl

Downing, J. (Photographer). (2009, February 21). *bling* [digital image]. Retrieved from http://bit.ly/1vwLZGb

Dunnette, B. (Photographer). (2007, November 28). *Worship Me* [digital image]. Retrieved from http://bit.ly/1D05roF

Everett, V. (Photographer). (2008, November 4). *Questions?* [digital image]. Retrieved from http://bit.ly/1w6dBqz

Fox, R.J. (Photographer). (2013, March 4). *Emotional Mental Physical Domestic Violence Spousal Abuse Trauma Scars Self Portrait Done with foolproof app* [digital image]. Retrieved from http://bit.ly/12Fjxux

Ginucplathottam. (Photographer). (2014, September 15). *jibin_new.jpg* [digital image]. Retrieved from http://morguefile.com/archive/#/?q=motorcycle&sort=pop&photo_lib=morgueFile

Green, T. (Photographer). (2007, October 14). *Slack End* [digital image]. Retrieved from http://bit.ly/1A8Rxux

Guldi, J. (Photographer). (2007, April 24). *Endless grading of term papers* [digital image]. Retrieved from http://bit.ly/160esiL

Hotshot, O. (Photographer). (2009, November 17). *SLER11_17_09_005* [digital image]. Retrieved from https://www.flickr.com/photos/oliviahotshot/4113022563/in/photolist-

Hyde, R. (Photographer). (2012, April 24). *(16/52) Grade On!* [digital image]. Retrieved from http://bit.ly/1ywoVtg

Jensen, A. (Photographer). (2010, April 28). *IMAG0004.jpg* [digital image]. Retrieved from http://bit.ly/1D4jnxO

Jordan, B. (Photographer). (2013, August 31). *Caught Stealing* [digital image]. Retrieved from http://bit.ly/1Ga82Zj

Jordan, B. (Photographer). (2014, June 9). *Grammar Basics* [digital image]. Retrieved from https://www.flickr.com/photos/x1brett/14379766274/in/photolist

Kconnors. (Photographer). (2009, August 1). *DSC_0014.jpg* [digital image]. Retrieved from http://morguefile.com/archive/#/?q=classroom&sort=pop&photo_lib=morgueFile

Kobylanski, I. (Photographer). (2011, November 14). *Gasp* [digital image]. Retrieved from https://www.flickr.com/photos/iankobylanski/6351498700/in/phot olist-aFg6hh-6HFDm3-6Posco-6Poriu

Krebs, D. (Photographer). (2013, March 3). *Experiencing, Learning, Reflecting* [digital image]. Retrieved from http://bit.ly/1CZuS9T

Krzeszak, M. (Photographer). (2012, March 2). *problems* [digital image]. Retrieved from http://bit.ly/1CZGmdq

Leung, M. (Photographer). (2005, August 17). *DSC02378* [digital image]. Retrieved from https://www.flickr.com/photos/lester/34764913/in/photolist-45bp4-45bpg-45bpb-6xQ455-6bKPQy

Maya, C. (Photographer). (2010, November 10). *Share* [digital image]. Retrieved from http://bit.ly/1wTJxjp

Medina, D. (Photographer). (2014, April 20). *IMG_0001.jpg* [digital image]. Retrieved from http://morguefile.com/archive/#/?q=apple%20mouse&sort=pop&p hoto_lib=morgueFile

Mingasson, M. (Photographer). (2008, March 27). *Personal Ecosystem* [digital image]. Retrieved from http://bit.ly/1ucOZag

Pippalou. (Photographer). (2014, October 4). *DSCN4867.jpg* [digital image]. Retrieved from http://www.morguefile.com/archive/display/898989

Richter, I. (Photographer). (2010, July 22). *J. Crew Construction Sign #6* [digital image]. Retrieved from http://bit.ly/1Iqj3K9

Ross, S. (Photographer). (2008, January 2). *Grade cutoffs* [digital image]. Retrieved from http://bit.ly/1wa95Y2

Sebastiano. (Photographer). (2008, October 25). *zarowka1.jpg* [digital image]. Retrieved from http://morguefile.com/archive/#/?q=technology&sort=pop&photo_

124

lib=morgueFile

Shankbone, D. (Photographer). (2014, February 2). *Social Media Interaction 2014* [digital image]. Retrieved from http://bit.ly/1s4Iig4

S.h.u.t.t.e.r.b.u.g. (Photographer). (2009, August 9). *be present* [digital image]. Retrieved from https://www.flickr.com/photos/qjotennis/3807139534/in/photostream/

Simpson, E. (Photographer). (2007, December 1). *Break the rules!* [digital image]. Retrieved from http://bit.ly/1vFuFDJ

Stasiuk, T. (Photographer). (2011, August 20). *Do not fear failure* [digital image]. Retrieved from https://www.flickr.com/photos/zstasiuk/6065631472/in/photolist-aeZWUY-4g2ChV

Takeshi. (Photographer). (2013, May 28). *"If we make consistent effort, based on proper education, we can change the world."- Dalai Lama* [digital image]. Retrieved from http://bit.ly/1CZCpp5

Tegtmeyer, K. (Photographer). (2002, September 30). *"One who walks in another's tracks leaves no footprints."* [digital image]. Retrieved from http://bit.ly/1qlJXN8

TerBurg, S. (Photographer). (2013, June 6). *Bootcamp Business Model Canvas the Game, June 5-7 2013 in Amsterdam* [digital image]. Retrieved from http://bit.ly/1vFnr2y

U.S. Army Corps of Engineers. (Photographer). (2012, February 14). *USACE manages repairs to Camp Darby's Freedom Square* [digital image] Retrieved from http://bit.ly/1vADk5v

Waifer, X. (Photographer). (2007, August 1). *It's showtime!* [digital image]. Retrieved from https://www.flickr.com/photos/waiferx/1025178134/in/photolist-2yAiK5-jRYCne-72CxwB-dnoQH7-ecRCsD-koo8cc-oK5bJs

Wetwebwork. (Photographer). (2008, April 5). *Quality and Value* [digital image]. Retrieved from http://bit.ly/1A8Tt6g

Whologwhy. (Photographer). (2011, August 7). *PATOLA CONNECTION* [digital image]. Retrieved from http://bit.ly/1z0cVD0

Made in the USA
Coppell, TX
05 July 2020